Pursuing Equity

Navigating School Funding & Governance in Australia

Concepts, Application, & Outcomes with a Spotlight on Victoria

Bandara Bandaranayake, PhD

Copyright © 2024 Author Bandara Bandaranayake

First publishing, 2024

All rights reserved. No part of this publication may be reproduced, distributed, or transmitted in any form or by any means, including photocopying, recording, or other electronic or mechanical methods, without the prior written permission of the author, except in the case of brief quotations embodied in critical reviews and certain other non-commercial uses permitted by copyright law. For permission requests, email the author at the address below.

ISBN: 978-0-6452133-5-5

bandaranayakeb@gmail.com
Bandaranayake Consulting Services Pty Ltd
Melbourne, Australia

Dedication

To my two sons

Chamara and Chatura

What is this book all about?

This book provides a comprehensive evaluation of Australia's school funding and governance framework, enriched with a robust conceptual foundation and a focused analysis of its application and outcomes in Victoria. Drawing on the author's extensive experience spanning nearly two decades with the Victorian Department of Education (formerly the Department of Education and Training, DET), it offers a detailed empirical perspective on the subject.

Supported by balanced empirical evidence, the book highlights the complexities and dynamics involved in pursuing equity in educational provision in Australia. Readers are encouraged to delve deeper and critically engage with these insights to fully appreciate the challenges and nuances of achieving equitable educational outcomes.

This is an essential resource for education researchers, administrators, teachers, parents, and school council members.

Table of Contents

	What is This Book All About?	v
	Table of Contents	vii
	Acknowledgements	ix
1	Introduction and Book Structure	1

Part I: Pillars of the Foundation

2	An Overview of the Australian Education System	11
3	Economic Models influencing School Finance & Governance	23
4	Legislative Foundation Ruling School Financing and Governance	33
5	Australian Political Framework Influencing Education	43
6	Exploring Key Concepts of School Finance and Governance	51
7	Distinctive Contextual Factors Affecting Australian Education	61

Part II: Historical Outlook

8	Evolution of School Financing and Governance Policies in the State of Victoria	71
9	Evolution of Federal Government's Interventions in School Funding	79

Part III: Methods of Funding

10	Federal Funding Methods to Government and Non-Government Schools	91
11	State Government Funding Methods for Victorian Government Schools	99
12	State government Funding Methods to Victorian Non-Government Schools	107

Part IV: Structural Frame of Finance

13	Revenue Structure of Victorian Government Schools	117

| 14 | Expenditure Structure in Victorian Government Schools | 127 |
| 15 | Resourcing Teaching Force: Workforce Management in Victorian Government Schools | 133 |

Part V: Execution Blueprint

| 16 | Unveiling the School Governance Model in Victoria | 141 |
| 17 | Managing Financial and Operational Risks in Victorian Government Schools | 147 |

Part VI: Gloomy Horizon of Outcomes

18	School Autonomy: Challenges of Financial Management and Governance in Victoria	161
19	School Autonomy: Unanticipated Financial Irregularities and Unethical Practices in Victoria	169
20	School Autonomy in Victoria: Unanticipated Governance Challenges	179
21	Devolution Paradox: Trends of Bureaucratisation of School Leadership in Victoria	191

Part VII: Outcomes & Prospects

22	Advocating Fairness: Socio-Political Dynamics Shaping the Power Balance in Education	203
23	Assessing Educational Equity: School Funding Disparities and Unmet Expectations	221
24	Beyond the Norm: Uncovering the Key Drivers and Missing Links Shaping Modern Educational Performance	237
25	The Pursuit of Equity: Emerging Comparative Perspectives, and Concluding Comments	249

Appendices

| 1 | Bibliography | 265 |
| 2 | About the Author | 289 |

Acknowledgements

Many senior public officials often bury their accumulated knowledge and insights when they formally leave public service. I chose a different path, sharing my knowledge with the community even during my tenure, fully committed to and within the public service code of conduct. After leaving public service, I continued to conduct independent research in my areas of expertise, sharing my insights with a wider audience.

At this instance, I extend my gratitude to my public service colleagues who supported me in various ways during my public service career and afterward.

I acknowledge that this is a significant step forward from my earlier publication, "Taking the Mystery Out of School Financing in Victoria, Australia" (2015, National Council for Professors of Educational Administration, NCPEA Publications, Michigan). I am grateful for the initial support provided by several academics, including Theodore Creighton (Virginia Tech), Thomas Kersten (Roosevelt University), Brad Bizzell (Radford University), Gerald Burke (Monash University), and Karen Starr (Deakin University).

Even though I have not mentioned them by name, I would also like to express my sincere gratitude to the individuals who played instrumental roles in the completion of this publication.

I have heavily utilised publicly available information from the official websites of the Victorian Department of Education (previously Department of Education and Training, DET), the Australian Department of Education, the Australian Curriculum, Assessment and Reporting Authority (ACARA), the Australian Bureau of Statistics (ABS), and other online sources to update relevant information for this publication.

I welcome readers' reviews and suggestions. As Australian and Victorian school finance and governance policies and systems are rapidly evolving, readers' comments and any ongoing critical developments will be incorporated into future editions.

Bandara Bandaranayake
Melbourne
Australia
bandaranayakeb@gmail.com

Chapter 1

Introduction & Book Structure

Introduction

This book offers a comprehensive evaluation of the school funding and governance framework in Australia, navigating key concepts and applications while highlighting emerging outcomes, including concerns and their implications.

Victoria has emerged as a leader in innovative school funding models and devolved governance arrangements, with a strong emphasis on school choice and autonomy. Focusing on Victoria, this book provides insights into its pioneering approaches in school funding and governance and the lessons learned within the broader federal context of Australian education.

Author's Perspectives

This publication enriches the discourse on school funding and governance by offering balanced practical perspectives and insights grounded in real-world experience and empirical research. Drawing from the author's extensive involvement in the field—including years of advising, investigating, analysing, problem-solving, and learning from real-world scenarios within the Victorian Department of

Education — this book presents valuable intuitions. Utilising empirical methods such as observation, case studies, content analysis, bootstrapping statistics, ethnography, and secondary data analysis, it identifies and validates these perspectives. Readers are encouraged to plunge deeper and critically engage with these insights.

Conceptual Landscape

The debate on school funding and governance, both globally and in Australia, is ongoing, reflecting critical discussions on resource allocation, educational management, and equitable access to quality education. In Australia, this debate has been a focal point for the past five decades, drawing significant political attention and public interest. Central to these discussions is the fair distribution of funding among schools, addressing disparities between affluent and disadvantaged institutions.

In 1977, Graham Freudenberg, a Labor speechwriter to the late Prime Minister Robert Menzies and historian, perceptively noted that "the oldest, deepest, most poisonous debate in Australia" revolved around government aid to church schools, or private schools. This sentiment remains relevant today.

The 2012 Gonski Review Report sparked renewed debate by advocating for a national needs-based and sector-blind funding model. Discussions persist on the extent of government intervention in funding adequacy, alongside considerations of market-oriented reforms such as school choice and autonomy. Moreover, debates also focus on the suitability of government funding for both government and non-government schools, raising concerns about equity, fairness, and accountability.

Effective school governance plays an essential role in maximising the benefits of allocated funds. While school finance may seem technical and complex, it is crucial for school leaders, council members, teachers, parents, and stakeholders to have a basic understanding of funding principles, sources, and financial management procedures and systems. This knowledge is essential for active engagement in school governance. This publication aims to unpack and present complex technical details in a simple format, analysing their interrelationships and interdependencies in the journey to reach educational goals.

Additionally, this book offers the perspective of how school finance and governance are intertwined with broader economic models, political agendas, and contextual and social environmental factors in Australia. Contemporary economic models advocate for school autonomy, school choice, and the devolution of decision-making as powerful and essential frameworks to enhance educational performance and efficiency. However, this book raises questions and presents observations regarding the inherent risks, drawbacks, strengths, and weaknesses of devolved school financial management and governance models, reaching such expectations, with reference to the State of Victoria.

Eventually, the importance lies in evaluating whether school funding and governance frameworks have contributed to advancing the quality of education and achieving equity and fairness. Initiatives like school choice, competition, and autonomy necessitate examining whether these frameworks advance equity or exacerbate inequality and whether they promote social segregation.

Chapter Structure

This chapter established the foundation for outlining the intents of this book. The subsequent section, comprising six chapters, delves into the Australian foundation where these concepts and processes are applied and progressed. Chapter two provides an overview of the Australian education system, including the country's demographic profile, school structure, and highlighting trends in growing a dual education system. Chapter three traces the ongoing influence of global economic trends on school finance and governance policies in Australia, exploring the trajectory from Keynesian to neoliberal paradigms. Chapter four presents the legislative framework governing education policies and distributing funds at federal and state levels, including key acts and regulations. Chapter five introduces the Australian political framework, enriched with powerful lobbying, and its influence on education policy agendas. It focuses on the leading parties, the Australian Labor Party and the Liberal Party of Australia. Chapter six introduces key concepts underlining school funding and governance e.g. education quality, funding adequacy, formula-based funding, equity, school choice, school autonomy and transparency. Chapter seven examines the unique contextual factors that shape and challenge Australian education on an ongoing basis. These factors include the abundance of rich natural resources, economic prosperity, political stability, colonial advantage, and migrant advantage, contrasted with the disadvantages faced by Indigenous communities.

Chapters eight and nine of the next part presents historical journey of the federal intervention in education funding and the growth of innovative school funding methods and governance arrangements in Victoria to date.

Chapter eight explores Victoria's pioneering role in school governance reforms, emphasising the shift towards formula-based school funding, while chapter nine traces the historical trajectory of the Commonwealth Government's influence on school financing, highlighting milestones like COAG initiatives, the Gonski proposals and the Australian Education Act 2013.

The chapters in the next part, 10, 11, and 12, present Federal and Victorian school funding methods, outlining the procedural setup for school funding. Chapter 10 explains federal funding methods for government and non-government schools, aligned with the principles of the Australian Education Act 2013. Chapter 11 presents Victorian government funding methods to government schools under School Resource Package (SRP) including student-based, school-based funding and targeted initiatives. The chapter 12 explains State government funding methods for non-government schools in Victoria, categorised into core funding and need-based funding.

Chapters 13, 14 and 15 of the next part reflects on school finance base in Government schools in Victoria. Chapter 13 sets out revenue structure of Victorian Government schools, covering state and Commonwealth grants along with other specific revenue sources available under school autonomy. Chapter 14 explains the expenditure structure for Victorian government schools, including recurrent and capital expenditure providing an understanding of how the money is being spent for local needs under school autonomy. Chapter 15 holds significant importance as it reveals the recruiting and management of the teaching force within government schools that help to operate autonomously. It centres on independence in effective workforce planning, recruitment, and maintenance of a robust school staff profile aimed at achieving local strategic goals at individual school levels.

The subsequent section (chapters 16 and 17) delves into the implementation of the school governance model in Victoria, which serves as the execution blueprint. Chapter 16 interprets the Victorian devolved school management system, defining governance arrangements and the functions under school councils. Chapter 17 describes the process of school financial and operational management within autonomy, encompassing strategies for mitigating financial and operational risks and ensuring transparency and accountability.

The next section, which includes chapters 18, 19, 20, and 21, discusses the emerging results and implications of the Victorian school finance and governance approach. This section outlines a bleak outlook in contrast to expectations, with the information primarily based on empirical evidence. Chapter 18 presents challenges encountered by government schools under autonomy. Chapter 19 highlights unanticipated outcomes in some schools including reported financial irregularities and unethical practices under the operations of school autonomy. Chapter 20 goes one step further to highlight governance challenges of school autonomy in Victorian government schools. Chapter 21 raises the possibility of creating a devolution paradox where school autonomy strengthened a central control and bureaucratic norms potentially undermining the school level educational leadership and teaching and learning process.

The final section, comprising chapters 22, 23, 24, and 25, explores the outcomes, implications, and prospects. Chapter 22 examines the persistent socio-political forces that shape the power balance within Australian education, subsequently influencing the frameworks for advancing school finance and governance agendas over time. Chapter 23 provides valuable insights into the effectiveness of school funding and governance initiatives as they progress within the backdrop of Australia's socio-economic footing. Chapter 24 aims to highlight key drivers and missing links shaping modern educational performance that operate outside the norm of the school funding and governance agenda, for our consideration. The final chapter (Chapter 25) seeks to connect the empirical evidence gathered in this study with broader research findings and perspectives on school funding and school governance under school choice and autonomy, culminating in concluding remarks and future prospects.

Part I

Pillars of Foundation: Establishing the Framework & Context

Chapter 2

An Overview of the Australian Education System

Introduction

This chapter offers an overview of the education system, starting with the composition of the Australian Federation, demographic profiles, and school structure. It delves into the two main school sectors, government and non-government (Catholic and independent schools), providing details of their compositions. Additionally, it discusses the trends of the growing dual education system, and its implications for education policy and funding interventions.

Composition of States and Territories

The Commonwealth (Federation) of Australia consists of six States and two Territories - New South Wales (NSW), Queensland (Qld), South Australia (SA), Tasmania (TAS), Victoria (VIC), Western Australia (WA), the Australian Capital Territory (ACT), and the Northern Territory (NT). There are three levels of Australian Government: Australian (Federal/Commonwealth), State/Territory, and local. The head of the Australian Government is a Prime Minister, while the State Governments are headed by Premiers and Territory Governments are headed by Chief Ministers.

New South Wales was the first Australian state to be established. It originated as a British penal colony in 1788 when Captain Arthur Phillip arrived with the First Fleet and established a settlement in Sydney Cove. Over time, the colony expanded and attracted free settlers, leading to its development as a British colony. Victoria was originally part of the colony of New South Wales. However, due to the rapid population growth and economic development resulting from the gold rush in the 1850s, Victoria became a separate colony in 1851. It was named after Queen Victoria. Queensland was initially part of the colony of New South Wales. It separated from New South Wales and became a separate colony in 1859, primarily due to the geographical and economic differences between the coastal areas and the inland regions. Queensland was named after Queen Victoria. South Australia was founded as a planned British colony in 1836. It was established as a free settlement and intended to provide greater freedom and equality compared to the penal colonies.

The Colony of Western Australia (also known as Swan River Colony) was established as a free colony on 2 May 1829 when Captain Fremantle formally took possession of the land of Western Australia in the name of the King of England. The Western Australia Act 1929 received Royal Assent in England on 14 May 1829 confirming the settlement as a British colony. It was initially a free settlement, attracting migrants seeking economic opportunities, particularly in agriculture and mining. Tasmania, formerly known as Van Diemen's Land, was initially established as a penal colony in 1803. It served as a British penal settlement for convicts, but later became a free colony. Tasmania was renamed in 1856 and became a self-governing colony. Australian Capital Territory was created in 1911 as the location for the new federal capital, Canberra. It was established on land that was formerly part of New South Wales. The Northern Territory was initially part of South Australia, but in 1911 it was transferred to federal control. It remained under direct federal administration until 1978 when it gained self-government.

Each state and territory have its own unique history, cultural heritage, and governance arrangements, contributing to the diverse nature of Australia's political and administrative landscape. Australian colonies unified to become a Federation in 1901.

Demographic Profile of Education

Australia's population reached 26.6 million by June 2023, marking a steady growth of around 1.4% annually over the past three decades, up from 17.6 million in June 1993. The primary driver of this growth has been net overseas migration, accounting for over half of the total population increase, while natural increase (births minus deaths) contributed the remaining portion.

Over time, Australia's population has aged, with the median age rising from 33.0 years in June 1993 to 38.3 years in June 2023. The proportion of individuals aged 65 and over has also seen a notable increase, rising from 12% to 17% during the same period.

Australia's population is predominantly concentrated in major cities, housing 73% of the total population. Approximately one-quarter (26%) resides in inner and outer regional areas, while the remainder (2%) resides in remote and very remote areas.

The population of Australia is characterised by its diversity. In 2022, 29.5% of the population was born overseas, with nearly half (48%) having at least one parent born overseas. Additionally, the Aboriginal and Torres Strait Islander (First Nations) population constituted 3.8% of the total Australian population as of June 2021, totalling 984,000 individuals based on ABS data.

In 2023, Australia boasted a total student enrollment of 4,086,998 across 9,629 schools. This student body represents approximately 17% of the total population, reflecting the typical age range of 5 to 19 years for school attendance. In the same period, there were 254,710 full-time Aboriginal and Torres Strait Islander students enrolled in schools throughout Australia. This demographic segment comprises roughly 5-6% of the total student population.

Australia's Schooling System

The Australian school system is a comprehensive education system that provides education to children and young people from preschool to secondary school. Education is compulsory for all children in Australia from the age of 6 to 17, with some variations between states and territories.

The Australian education system is broadly structured as follows:
1. Preschool: years 3 to 5
2. primary school: seven or eight years, starting at Foundation (also called kindergarten/ preparatory/ pre-school) through to Year 6 or 7
3. secondary school: four years from Years 7 or 8 to 10
4. senior secondary school: two years from Years 11 to 12
5. tertiary education: includes higher education and vocational education and training (VET).

Preschool education, also known as kindergarten or pre-primary, is offered to children aged 3 to 5 years. It is not compulsory but is widely available and plays an important role in preparing children for formal schooling. Primary education covers the early years of schooling from approximately 5 to 12 years of age. It typically includes grades or year levels from Foundation/Prep/Kindergarten to Year 6 or 7, depending on the state or territory. Secondary education follows primary education and generally includes grades or year levels from Year 7 or 8 to Year 12. It prepares students for further study or entry into the workforce.

Primary schools consist of Pre-Year 1 to year 6, and secondary schools consist of year 7 to year 12 in New South Wales, Victoria, Tasmania, Northern Territory and Australian Capital Territory. Primary schooling years consist of pre-Year 1 to Year 7, and secondary schools from Year 8 to Year 12 in Queensland, South Australia and Western Australia.

Education systems at each State/Territory are managed by State/Territory education authorities. For example, the Victorian education system is administered by the State's Department of Education and Training (DET). The Department provides education and development services to children, young people and adults both directly through government schools and indirectly through regulation and funding of early childhood services, non-government schools and training.

Regulation of Schools

In Australia, both government and non-government schools are to be registered to operate officially. The registration ensures that schools meet certain standards related to good governance, strong financial management, effective curriculum, sound teaching practice, a safe environment for children as specified by state legislation or regulations.

Each state and territory has its own education department or authority responsible for overseeing the registration process. Schools seeking registration must typically demonstrate compliance with relevant education laws, regulations, and standards set by the respective education authority. This often involves providing detailed information about the school's curriculum, staffing, governance structure, facilities, and policies.

School Sectors

The term 'sector' is used to differentiate between the main types of schools in Australia. The Australian schooling system is divided into three sectors, each having a significant enrollment share.

Government School Sector

The government school sector in Australia operates on the principle of equal rights for all citizens. The education provided in government schools is free, compulsory, and secular. State and territory governments are responsible for managing the education policies and administration of government schools.

Victoria started registering government schools as well since the Education and Training Reform Act 2006. As mentioned previously, these functions are performed by the State and Territory Departments of Education. Even though education is free for students attending government schools the State Governments have developed a policy to charge a modest fee, which is not compulsory. Even as the sector is being traditionally centralised in the allocation of resources and management of schools, processes have changed over the recent decades.

Government schools cater to a large proportion of educationally disadvantaged students - indigenous Australians. For example, 85 percent of the indigenous students, 78 percent of students with disability, 83 percent of students from remote and very remote areas, and 79 percent bottom quarter of the socio economic advantage are in the government school sector (Gonski, et al, 2011).

Non-Government School Sector

Non-Government school is a school registered to provide education in a state or territory which is not owned or operated by the state or territory government. Also known as a 'private' school. There are two types of non-government schools in Australia, Catholic and independent.

Catholic Schools

The Catholic education sector refers to the school education provided by the Roman Catholic Church of Australia within the Australian education system. In 1879, the Catholics Bishops of Australia released a *Joint Pastoral Letter* stating that Catholic families must send their children to a Catholic school, to ensure that their children receive religious education. Since then, the Catholic education system has grown to be the second biggest sector following the government school sector, in Australia. Approximately 96 percent of the Catholic schools are members of the Catholic school systems.

Catholic Education Commissions in Australia are bodies responsible for overseeing and supporting Catholic schools within their respective regions or dioceses. These commissions typically operate at both the state and diocesan levels and play a crucial role in the governance, administration, and strategic direction of Catholic education. Key functions of Catholic Education Commissions include, policy development, funding allocation, pastoral care, professional development, advocacy and community development. Each Catholic Education Commission operates within the framework of Catholic teachings and values while also adhering to relevant education laws and regulations in Australia. These commissions contribute significantly to the provision of high-quality Catholic education and the overall educational landscape in the country.

Independent Schools

Independent schools in Australia operate autonomously from the government education system and are governed by a combination of legislation, regulations, and governance structures. Independent schools have significant autonomy in decision-making regarding curriculum, staffing, finances, and overall school management. They are typically governed by a board of directors, or a council composed of parents, community members, and educational professionals. Each state and territory has regulatory bodies responsible for overseeing the registration and compliance of independent schools. These bodies ensure that independent schools meet the necessary standards and operate in accordance with the law. In Victoria, independent schools are to be not-for-profit institutions.

Traditionally, independent schools had been established by wealthy families or community groups for particular schooling needs, but not always with religious affiliations.

The Australian independent schools differ slightly from those of the United States, as the Australian government provides funds to all schools, including independent schools, on a need-based formula (details are provided in the subsequent chapters). Most of the original independent schools in Australia are Schools affiliated with Christian denominations, comprising of Baptist, Anglican, Lutheran, Methodist, Presbyterian, and Seventh-day Adventist schools. In addition different groups of independent schools have been included such as Non-denominational Christian schools, Islamic schools, Jewish schools, Montessori schools, Rudolf Steiner schools, Schools constituted under specific Acts of Parliament, such as grammar schools in some states, Community schools, Indigenous community schools, Schools that specialise in meeting the needs of students with disabilities, and Schools that cater for students at severe educational risk due to a range of social/ emotional/ behavioural and other risk factors (ISCA, 2017).

Forty-seven percent of the students from the top quarter socio economic advantage attend independent schools in Australia. Independent schools cater to five percent of indigenous students, six percent of students with disability and three percent of students from remote and very remote areas (Gonski, et al, 2011). This means that independent schools predominantly provide schooling to the affluent social class, in metropolitan areas.

Home Schooling

Homeschooling is another mode of schooling legally allowed in Victoria. The Education and Training Reform Act 2006 provides the legal framework for homeschooling in Victoria. Under this Act, parents who choose to homeschool must register their children with the Victorian Registration and Qualifications Authority (VRQA) and ensure that the education provided meets Australian curriculum standards. The Act mandates that parents submit an annual learning plan outlining the educational objectives, methods, and resources they will use to educate their children at home, safeguarding the quality of home education and ensuring it meets the necessary educational outcomes.

In recent years, homeschooling has become a significant mode of education in Victoria, with over 8,733 students registered in 2021 (myhomeschool.com). This increase reflects a broader trend driven by dissatisfaction with traditional schooling systems, concerns about bullying, and the desire for a curriculum that aligns with family values and beliefs. The COVID-19 pandemic has further accelerated this trend, as parents have become more involved in their children's education and recognised the benefits of a home-based learning environment. While homeschooling offers a flexible and personalised educational experience, it also presents challenges such as the need for significant parental involvement and the potential for social isolation. To mitigate these challenges, many homeschooling families in Victoria participate in co-ops and support groups that provide social interaction and shared learning experiences.

Growing Dual School System

In 2022, 64.5 percent of the students attended government (public) schools and the remaining 35 percent attended non-government (private) schools. The non-government schools included Catholic schools, educating approximately 19.7 percent of the students, and independent schools, educating approximately 15.9 percent of the students.

Figure 1: Composition of the Australian schooling system

	Number of schools		Number of students	
	2002	2022	2002	2022
Government	72.3	69.9 (-2.4)	68.4	64.5 (-3.9)
Catholic	17.7	18.4 (+0.7)	19.9	19.7 (-0.2)
Independent	10.0	11.5 (+1.5)	11.7	15.9 (+4.2)
Total	**100**	**100**	**100**	**100**

(Source – ACRA and ABS, *Schools*, 2024)

As shown in figure 1, it is not only that the non-government school sector is proportionately high in Australia but it is also continuously growing. The government school sector appears to be gradually shrinking. In contrast to OECD countries, Australia currently exhibits a notable prevalence of non-government schools. The average distribution in OECD countries was 82 percent publicly managed schools and 18 percent privately managed schools. Importantly, the non-government school sector in Australia is on a steady growth trajectory.

Today, Australia maintains a dual system comprising government and non-government schools, with funding allocated to both sectors. Ongoing debates focus on striking the appropriate balance between public and private education and ensuring the equitable distribution of resources.

Chapter 3

Economic Models Influencing School Finance & Governance

Introduction

School finance and governance policies in Australia have been profoundly influenced by global economic trends. This chapter delves into Australia's economic trajectory since World War II, examining the interplay between Keynesian and neoliberal policies. Currently, a apparent shift towards post-modern conservatism or post-neoliberalism is emerging. Despite these shifts, dualism characterised by a blend of social democracy persists within the Australian economic framework.

Era of Keynesian Economics

Keynesian economic policies were introduced during the Great Depression of the 1930s and became more pronounced during and after World War II (Keynes, 1936; Blinder, 1988)). This era marked a significant shift in economic strategy, characterised by increased government intervention to manage demand and ensure economic stability. Keynesian principles advocated for counter-cyclical measures to dampen economic downturns and spur growth during recessions. In Australia, these ideas influenced fiscal policies like taxation, government spending, and public investment.

Central to Keynesian thought is the pursuit of full employment, which shaped labour regulations, welfare programs, and job initiatives in Australia. Policies such as minimum wage laws, job creation programs, and unemployment benefits were implemented to provide opportunities for all willing and able workers. Keynesian economics also supported social welfare programs to aid vulnerable groups and reduce income inequality. In Australia, these policies led to the establishment and expansion of safety nets in healthcare, education, housing, and income support, fostering social cohesion and reducing poverty. Public investment in infrastructure was another crucial aspect, translating into significant investments across sectors like transportation, energy, and telecommunications, creating jobs and enhancing long-term competitiveness.

Impact on Education

Keynesian economic policies had a profound effect on education, emphasising government investment in the sector. During times of economic expansion, substantial funds were allocated to education infrastructure, teacher training programs, and educational reforms. This investment aimed to enhance human capital formation, foster innovation, and improve the overall quality of education.

Keynesian-inspired policies played a pivotal role in expanding access to education and promoting equity in educational opportunities (Carnoy & Levin, 1985). Increased government spending facilitated the establishment of new schools, the provision of scholarships, and financial assistance programs, and the implementation of policies aimed at reducing socioeconomic disparities in education outcomes. This inclusivity aligned with Keynesian ideals of promoting social welfare and reducing inequalities.

While Keynesian policies yielded positive outcomes for education, they also faced challenges and criticisms. Critics argued that excessive government intervention could lead to inefficiencies, bureaucratic red tape, and distortions in resource allocation within the education sector. Additionally, fluctuations in government spending cycles could result in uncertainty and instability for educational institutions, impacting long-term planning and sustainability.

Era of Neoliberal Economic Policies

The rise of neoliberal economic policies in the 1970s was a response to economic challenges such as stagflation. Critics of Keynesianism, notably the Chicago School of Economics led by figures like Milton Friedman and Friedrich Hayek, argued that excessive government intervention, high taxes, and rigid labour markets stifled economic growth and innovation (Friedman, 1962; Hayek, 1960). Neoliberalism, advocating for free markets, limited government involvement, and deregulation, gained traction amid growing global interconnectedness facilitated by technological advancements.

In Australia, neoliberal policies gained prominence in the 1980s and 1990s. Deregulation initiatives were evident across sectors like finance, telecommunications, and labour markets. For instance, the liberalisation of the financial sector in the 1980s eliminated many restrictions on banking and financial services. Additionally, privatisation efforts saw state-owned enterprises like Telstra and airports transition to private ownership.

Neoliberalism emphasises fiscal discipline, prompting austerity measures to curb budget deficits and public debt, often resulting in cuts to social welfare, healthcare, and education. Trade liberalisation was pursued through agreements like the Australia-United States Free Trade Agreement and the Comprehensive and Progressive Agreement for Trans-Pacific Partnership. Labor market reforms aimed to foster flexibility by decentralising wage setting, promoting enterprise bargaining, and reducing union influence.

While neoliberal policies bolstered economic growth, productivity, and international competitiveness in Australia, they faced criticism for widening income inequality, weakening social safety nets, and prioritising market outcomes over social welfare concerns.

Impact on Education

Neoliberal policies have significantly impacted the education system, prioritising consumerist values over educational equity and resulting in a stratified system. Angus (2015) argues that these policies support socio-political contexts that favour market-driven principles, highlighting how the rhetoric of choice and freedom often obscures the resulting socio-economic divides.

Neoliberal education policies are marked by a shift towards market-driven principles, privatisation, competition, and reduced state involvement (Ball, 2012). These policies often champion school choice, enabling parents to select between public and private schools, viewing education as a market commodity. This fosters competition among schools, advocating for institutions to vie for students and funding.

Decentralisation is a key aspect, granting greater autonomy to individual schools and increasing local authority over curriculum and management decisions. The marketisation of education promotes competition, choice, and consumerism. Initiatives like charter schools and voucher programs introduce market dynamics into education. In Australia, policies supporting school autonomy and parental choice have diversified educational options and boosted private and independent schools.

Privatisation is encouraged through outsourcing educational services, founding private schools, and implementing public-private partnerships (PPPs). Private schools thrive under neoliberalism, attracting government support and catering to families seeking alternatives to public education. Neoliberal economic principles influence funding models, with a shift towards formula-based and performance-based funding tied to student achievement, school performance, and market demand. This prompts debates over resource allocation, equity, and distribution between public and private schools, and disadvantaged and advantaged communities.

Deregulation and accountability measures are promoted, focusing on outcomes-based accountability, standardised testing, and school performance metrics. In Australia, initiatives like NAPLAN and the My School website emphasise transparency and accountability.

Neoliberal economic policies have significantly altered Australia's education landscape, reshaping funding models, governance structures, and educational priorities. While proponents tout market-oriented reforms for promoting efficiency, innovation, and choice, critics highlight concerns about equity, social justice, and the commodification of education. The ongoing debate over the market's role in education continues to shape policy discussions and the future trajectory of Australia's education system.

Emerging Trend of Post-Neoliberalism

As the influence of neoliberal economic policies wanes in some contexts, post-neoliberal economic policies are emerging, bringing new perspectives and priorities to the forefront. Post-neoliberalism represents a departure from the strict adherence to neoliberal economic policies and emphasises a more balanced approach that addresses social, environmental, and economic concerns (Peck, & Theodore, 2015; Crouch, C. 2011).

Key Economic Aspects of Post-Neoliberalism

Social Welfare: Post-neoliberalism aims to reduce inequalities through progressive taxation, wealth redistribution, and social spending. This includes policies to provide universal healthcare, education, housing, and social security.

- Environmental Sustainability: Recognising the importance of environmental sustainability, post-neoliberalism aims to integrate environmental concerns into economic decision-making. This involves promoting renewable energy, sustainable resource management, and measures to mitigate climate change.

- Government Regulation: Post-neoliberalism advocates for a re-evaluation of the role of government in regulating markets and addressing market failures. It supports public investment in infrastructure, education, healthcare, and other essential services as a means to stimulate economic growth, create employment, and enhance social well-being.

- Community Participation and Democratic Decision-Making: Post-neoliberalism emphasises the importance of community participation and democratic decision-making in economic governance. This involves empowering local communities, workers, and other stakeholders to have a voice in economic decision-making processes.

- Global Economic System: Post-neoliberalism advocates for a more equitable and inclusive global economic system that addresses the needs and concerns of developing countries, marginalised communities, and future generations. This includes reforming international trade and finance systems to promote fair trade, debt relief, and global economic stability.

- Inclusive Development: Post-neoliberalism involves implementing policies to reduce poverty, unemployment, and social exclusion, and promoting inclusive development strategies.

Impact on Education

Post-neoliberal economic models acknowledge the increasing demand for education policies that foster equity and inclusivity. Efforts may target reducing educational disparities, tackling socio-economic inequalities, and ensuring universal access to quality education. There's a shift towards holistic education, moving beyond standardised testing to cultivate well-rounded individuals. Moreover, education policies may embrace global citizenship education, preparing students for active engagement in a globally interconnected world (Robertson, et. al 2015).

Post-neoliberal economic policies prioritise reinvesting in public education, recognising it as a vital public good crucial for social cohesion and economic prosperity. This involves boosting government funding for public schools, addressing infrastructure gaps, reducing class sizes, and enhancing teacher training and support. Strengthening the public education system aims to guarantee equitable access to high-quality education for all, regardless of socio-economic status.

Post-neoliberal approaches challenge the dominance of privatisation and marketisation in education, emphasising public accountability, democratic governance, and community involvement. This may entail restraining the expansion of private schools, limiting the influence of for-profit educational providers, and fostering collaboration between public and private institutions.

Equity-cantered funding models are advocated, prioritising the alleviation of socio-economic disparities and educational inequalities. Implementing needs-based funding formulas based on student need and school disadvantage is proposed. Additionally, reducing reliance on performance-based funding mechanisms that exacerbate inequities and foster competition between schools is emphasised.

Post-neoliberal economic policies promote democratic governance structures and community engagement mechanisms, empowering stakeholders to participate in decision-making processes. Strengthening school councils, establishing parent and community advisory committees, and fostering partnerships between schools and community organisations aim to enhance transparency, accountability, and responsiveness to community needs.

Overall, post-neoliberal economic policies are reshaping Australia's education landscape by challenging neoliberalism's market-driven approach and prioritising equity, social justice, and democratic governance. Some foresee a potential shift towards a more egalitarian society.

Continued Trends of Dualism and Social Democracy

Dualism

In reality, both in Australia and globally, there is no strict adherence to either Keynesian or neoliberal economic policies. Even as new paradigms emerge, it's unlikely that post-neoliberal policies will completely replace existing ones. Instead, elements of each model may persist alongside emerging trends.

Dualism, in this context, refers to the coexistence of multiple economic processes or markets within the same framework. For example, Keynesian fiscal policies like government spending and taxation for demand management persist alongside principles advocating public investment and government intervention for economic stability. Similarly, neoliberal emphasis on market mechanisms persists, albeit with adjustments to ensure broader societal benefits. As globalisation continues, there may be a shift towards policies addressing contemporary challenges such as climate change, technological disruptions, and social inequality.

Social Democracy

Australia's governance reflects a blend of social democracy and market-driven principles, incorporating both welfare state elements and liberal economic policies (Maddison, et. al. 2013; Latham, 2001). Often labelled as a social democracy, Australia boasts a mixed-market economy, underpinned by various social democratic features.

Australia's commitment to social equity is reflected in its robust welfare state. Medicare provides universal healthcare, subsidising medical services and pharmaceuticals for all. Welfare provisions include income support, pensions, disability support, and family assistance. Education is accessible and affordable from primary to tertiary levels. A progressive taxation system redistributes wealth, with higher earners contributing more. Strong labour unions ensure fair wages and workplace rights. Policies promote social inclusion and combat discrimination, underscoring Australia's dedication to inclusivity.

Australia's social democratic model blends capitalism with a robust welfare state to achieve objectives like equality and social cohesion. However, the balance between market-oriented and welfare-focused policies may shift with changes in political landscapes and government priorities, reflecting the diversity of Australia's political framework. An account of the Australian political framework is presented in a separate chapter.

Chapter 4

Legislative Foundation Ruling School Financing & Governance.

Introduction

Chapter four outlines the legislative framework governing education policies and school funding at both federal and state levels in Australia. Only the key legislation applicable to the subject matter in this publication is captured. It examines the evolution of legislation influenced by colonial heritage, economic models, and the growing dualism of social democracy. This chapter begins with a focus on the Education Act 1872 (Victoria), which established the foundation for school funding and the dual education system.

The Education Act 1872

From 1872 to 1895, Australian colonies addressed education challenges by enacting legislation for free, compulsory, and secular education. These included the Education Act 1872 (VIC), The Public Schools Amendment Act 1873 (TAS), The Education Act 1875 (SA), State Education Act 1875 (QLD), Public Instruction Act 1880 (NSW), and The Elementary Education Act 1871 Amendment Act 1894 (WA).

The Education Act (Vic) of 1872 marked Victoria as the first Australian colony to institute a centralised public school system based on the principles of free, secular, and compulsory education. With the passage of the Education Act in 1872, all children aged 6-15 were mandated to attend school, unless they could provide a reasonable excuse. Financial support to church schools ceased in 1874, allowing these institutions to operate independently. The establishment of the Education Act also gave rise to the Department of Education, led by Victoria's inaugural Minister of Education.

The Act made education secular, compulsory, and free. Through one Act of Parliament, Victoria appeared to come closest to what was eventually thought of as the Australian Settlement in Education (Campbell and Proctor, 2014). To reach a point where the principles of the Education Act 1872 were achieved, it required advances in the secular and liberal conceptions of the state and modern citizenship.

The Education Act 1872 established a system where public funds were not to be given to schools that chose to remain independent of the state-run school system. The Act created a dual education system, with public schools funded by the government and non-governmental schools or schools with religious affiliations relying on self-funding. The Victorian model did not prevent Catholic Bishops of Australia from establishing their own Catholic School System. In 1879, Catholic Bishops enabled Catholic families to adhere to a decree stating that the children of all Catholic families must regularly attend Catholic schools. This was mainly to avoid Catholic children enrolling in public schools.

Figure 2: Expansion of Free, Secular, and Compulsory Education Systems in Australian States

State	Compulsory Schooling	Free Education	Secular Education	No Funds to Religious Schools	Central Control
Victoria	1872	1872	1872	1872	1872
NSW	1880	1906	1880	1882	1880
QLD	1900	1870	1875	1880	1875
WA	1871	1901	1895	1895	1893
SA	1875	1892	1852	1851	1875
Tasmania	1868	1908	1854	1854	1885

(Source: Campbell, C., & Proctor, H. 2014).

The Education and Training Reform Act 2006

The Education and Training Reform Act 2006 in Victoria, Australia, represents a significant piece of legislation aimed at reforming and modernising the education and training system in the state. The Act governs education and training within the state and establishes the legal framework for the provision of education, including schools, universities, vocational education, and training.

The Act establishes compulsory education requirements, stating that children between the ages of 6 and 17 must attend school or participate in an approved education or training program unless exempted. The Act outlines the governance and administration of government schools, including the establishment and management of school councils. It defines the roles and responsibilities of principals, teachers, and other staff members.

The Act defines the governance structure for government schools and establishes School Councils as key decision-making bodies. It outlines the roles and responsibilities of School Councils in school management, including financial management, strategic planning, and community engagement. The Act also emphasises the importance of accountability and transparency in school operations.

The Act provides the framework for curriculum and assessment in schools. It sets out the minimum standards for student learning, including the development of key skills and knowledge across various subject areas. The Act establishes the Victorian Registration and Qualifications Authority (VRQA) responsible for regulating education and training providers in Victoria. It outlines the regulatory framework for registration, accreditation, and compliance monitoring to maintain quality standards and safeguard the interests of students and the community.

The Act recognises the importance of parent and community engagement in education. It encourages schools to foster partnerships with parents, caregivers, and the broader community to enhance student learning outcomes and school effectiveness.

The Constitution of Australia 1901

The Constitution of Australia, enacted in 1901, serves as the supreme law governing the Commonwealth of Australia, outlining the framework for its system of government. While the Constitution does not explicitly mention schools or education, the Commonwealth government has exerted significant influence over education through reinterpretation and the development of new legislation, leveraging its fiscal authority over the states.

Education, including school funding and provision, is considered a residual power under section 51 of the

Constitution, primarily resting with the State Governments. However, by the late twentieth and early twenty-first centuries, the Federal government emerged as a major funder of Australian education at all levels, shaping policy and legislation in the process.

Australia's participation in wars during the early 20th century necessitated national efforts, including education and training, leading to increased Federal support and intervention in areas such as research and military capacity development. Section 96 of the Constitution, allowing the Parliament to grant financial assistance to states, became a cornerstone of ambitious Commonwealth policies, including education. Following World War II, the Commonwealth government's expanded taxation powers led to increased funding for various purposes, including education, despite initial disagreements with some conditions attached to funding.

In 1966, the Commonwealth established its Department of Education and Science, marking increased federal intervention in education. The 1960s migration fuelled school system growth, leading to financial pressures on non-government schools and the establishment of the Australian Schools Commission under the Whitlam government. The High Court's 1981 ruling clarified that Commonwealth assistance to religious schools did not violate the Constitution's prohibition against establishing religion. This tension is detailed in a forthcoming chapter

Australian Education Act 2013

After the Gonski Review report of 2012, the Labor Government formulated the National Plan for School Improvement (NPSI), aimed at achieving specific educational objectives by 2025 and implementing a funding scheme to support these goals. Enshrined within the Australian Education Act 2013, this plan represented the government's vision for the future of Australian education, becoming enforceable from January 1, 2014.

The Act's primary objectives include ensuring a high-quality and equitable education system for all students, lifting educational attainment rates, narrowing achievement gaps, and implementing a needs-based funding model. The legislation emphasises that every student deserves an excellent education regardless of their background or circumstances, fostering a system that enables all students to reach their full potential. Additionally, it recognises the vital role of diverse stakeholders, including governments, education authorities, parents, and community organisations, in delivering quality education.

To address funding disparities and ensure fair resource allocation, the Act introduces the Schooling Resource Standard (SRS) and establishes the National School Resourcing Board (NSB), emphasising the importance of coordinated efforts between state and federal governments for successful implementation. The SRS defines the minimum funding required for quality education, considering various student and school factors, while the NSB oversees funding arrangements to uphold the Act's principles.

The Education Regulations 2023

The Education Regulations 2023 serve as the regulatory framework for the Education Act 2013, encompassing a comprehensive set of rules governing various facets of the education sector in Australia. These regulations, updated as of 2023, cover a wide range of areas essential for maintaining high standards in education.

Key aspects of Australian education regulations include:

- Curriculum Standards: These regulations outline the curriculum requirements for different education levels, ensuring alignment with national standards.
- Teacher Qualifications and Registration: Criteria for teacher qualifications and registration are established, including educational credentials and professional certifications.
- School Governance and Administration: Regulations govern the establishment, operation, and governance of educational institutions, including public and private schools.
- Student Welfare and Protection: Regulations focus on student welfare, safety, and protection within educational environments.
- Funding and Resource Allocation: Regulations govern the allocation of funding and resources to educational institutions, ensuring equitable distribution and support for educational priorities and initiatives.
- Compliance and Monitoring: Mechanisms for monitoring compliance with education standards are established, with oversight bodies responsible for enforcement and inspections to address non-compliance.
- Quality Assurance and Accreditation: Provisions for quality assurance and accreditation processes assess and recognise the quality of educational programs and institutions.

Australian education regulations maintain standards, ensure compliance, and safeguard the interests of students, educators, and the broader community.

The Corporations Act 2001 and Other Legislations

The Corporations Act 2001 in Australia mainly governs the regulation of corporations, including not-for-profit organisations like independent schools structured as companies limited by guarantee. This legal framework ensures governance, financial management, and liability protection while ensuring compliance with regulatory standards. Independent schools, as incorporated entities under this Act, must adhere to corporate governance requirements, establish boards of directors, and maintain financial transparency through annual reporting and audits.

Directors of independent school boards have fiduciary duties to act in the school's best interests, overseeing strategic direction, financial management, and operational performance. While the Act provides limited liability protection for directors and officers, they can still be held personally liable for breaches, emphasising the importance of diligent governance.

Additionally, independent and Catholic schools must comply with corporate governance and auditing legislation at both federal and state/territory levels. The Australian Charities and Not-for-profits Commission (ACNC) Act 2012 regulates charities, including many schools operating as charitable organisations. Each jurisdiction may have its own laws covering areas like board composition and transparency, with schools often adhering to governance codes and standards developed by educational authorities or industry bodies.

Financial auditing is mandatory for transparency and accountability, with requirements set by the ACNC Act 2012 and state/territory regulations. Auditing standards are established by the Australian Auditing Standards Board (AUASB) to ensure compliance with international standards. Independent and Catholic schools in Australia must comply with corporate governance and auditing legislation to ensure effective management and accountability.

Laws Against Discrimination and Ensuring Equitable Educational Opportunities

In Australia, several laws are designed to ensure equal access to education and provide mechanisms for parents and students to take legal action against education departments or schools for issues such as discrimination and the failure to provide equitable educational opportunities.

- **Disability Discrimination Act 1992 (DDA):** This act prohibits discrimination against people with disabilities in various areas, including education. Complaints can be filed with the Australian Human Rights Commission (AHRC).
- **Equal Opportunity Act 2010 (Victoria) and Similar Acts in Other States and Territories**: These acts prohibit discrimination based on attributes such as race, gender, disability, and age in education and other areas. Complaints can be lodged with the Equal Opportunity Commission or Anti-Discrimination Board of the respective state or territory.
- **Australian Education Act 2013**: This act sets the national policy and funding framework for Australian schools, emphasising equity and quality in education. Although primarily a funding framework, complaints

about inequitable treatment can be raised through state and territory education departments.

- **Racial Discrimination Act 1975**: This act prohibits discrimination based on race, colour, descent, or national or ethnic origin in various areas, including education. Complaints can be filed with the AHRC.
- **Sex Discrimination Act 1984**: This act prohibits discrimination based on sex, marital status, pregnancy, or potential pregnancy in various areas, including education. Complaints can be filed with the AHRC.
- **Human Rights Act 2004 (ACT) and Charter of Human Rights and Responsibilities Act 2006 (Victoria):** These acts protect various human rights, including the right to education and the right to be free from discrimination. Complaints can be lodged with the respective Human Rights Commissions.
- **Education and Training Reform Act 2006 (Victoria) and Similar Acts in Other States and Territories:** These acts govern the operation and governance of schools, including standards of education and student welfare. Complaints can be raised with the Department of Education and Training or equivalent bodies. Ombudsman offices handle complaints regarding administrative actions of education departments.

If no resolution is reached through the complaint mechanisms provided by these agencies, legal action can be taken in tribunals or courts if necessary. These laws collectively ensure that students have access to equitable education opportunities and provide mechanisms for parents and students to seek redress in cases of discrimination or other forms of inequity in the education system.

Chapter 5

Australian Political Framework Influencing Education

Introduction

Chapter Five introduces the Australian political framework and its influence on education policies. It highlights the two main political parties, the Australian Labor Party (ALP) and the Liberal Party of Australia, which historically alternate in power and form the backbone of the country's political system. The chapter also notes the coalition between the Liberal Party and the National Party, which represents rural interests. Each party in Australia has distinct values, ideologies, and priorities that shape its approach to education policy, thereby influencing the development and direction of Australian education.

Political Process

Political parties undoubtedly play a pivotal role in attaining office, yet numerous other factors significantly influence governance and public policy formulation. Various interest groups spanning rural, commercial, industrial sectors, and diverse lobbying organisations advocate for a spectrum of government actions, from legislation to planning permissions and subsidies for various projects. Balancing these diverse demands while considering the public interest constitutes a major governmental challenge.

Both the ALP and the Liberal Party of Australia play significant roles in shaping education policies, albeit with different ideologies and approaches. The leaders of the major political parties, including the Prime Minister (if the party is in government) or the Leader of the Opposition (if the party is in opposition), often play a significant role in setting the agenda and direction of education policies. Parliamentary representatives, including ministers responsible for education portfolios, contribute to policy development and implementation through parliamentary debates, committee inquiries, and legislative processes.

Political parties develop education policies through a variety of mechanisms, including policy forums, party conferences, consultation with stakeholders (such as educators, parents, unions, and industry groups), expert advice, research, and internal party deliberations. Policy proposals may also be informed by election platforms, public opinion polling, and responses to emerging issues or challenges in education.

Political parties often engage in consultation and dialogue with relevant stakeholders to gather input, feedback, and perspectives on education policies. This can include meetings with education unions, professional associations, parent groups, school leaders, and education experts to inform policy development and ensure that proposals align with the needs and priorities of the education sector.

Education policies are prominently featured in election campaigns as parties seek to articulate their vision for education and gain public support for their proposals. Parties may release policy documents, make campaign promises, participate in debates, and engage in media interviews to communicate their education priorities and differentiate their positions from their opponents.

The Australian Labor Party (ALP)

The ALP traditionally aligns with social democratic principles, advocating for policies aimed at reducing social inequality, protecting workers' rights, and providing a strong social safety net. This includes support for universal healthcare (Medicare), public education, and social welfare programs. The ALP also tends to support progressive social policies, including marriage equality, gender equality, and multiculturalism. It often champions issues related to social justice, environmental sustainability, and human rights.

The ALP is one of the oldest political parties in Australia, with a history dating back to the late 19th century. Its formation and early development were influenced by the emerging Labor movement and the desire to represent the interests of the working class. The ALP is considered centre-left.

The ALP was officially founded in 1891. The principles of the ALP have evolved over time, reflecting the changing political landscape and societal priorities. These principles include:

- Social Justice: The ALP is committed to achieving social justice and reducing inequality. This includes policies aimed at improving access to education, healthcare, and social services.
- Workers' Rights: Historically rooted in the labour movement, the ALP advocates for workers' rights, fair

wages, and decent working conditions. This commitment remains central to the party's platform.
- Economic Reform: The party has embraced economic reform, including periods of economic modernisation and globalisation, and promotes mixed economic policies, including financial deregulation.
- Environmental Stewardship: In recent years, the ALP has increasingly emphasised environmental sustainability and the need for responsible environmental policies.
- Equality and Inclusion: The ALP has been a supporter of equality and inclusion, advocating for the rights of minority groups and marginalised communities.

The ALP's platform, often referred to as the National Platform, sets out its education and funding agenda. It states that public schools are among the nation's most important institutions and should be fully and fairly funded to deliver excellent secular education that meets the needs of every child. Labor believes parents have a right to choose a non-government school and that non-government schools should be supported by public funding that reflects need. Labor works with states and territories to implement a properly funded national needs-based and sector-blind school funding model, to ensure that:

- All schools are on a path to fair and full funding that meets the needs of all students.
- Disadvantaged schools get the biggest funding increases in the shortest time, tied to practical reforms.

The Liberal Party of Australia

The Liberal Party of Australia is rooted in classical liberalism, emphasising individual freedom, free markets, limited government intervention in the economy, and personal responsibility. It advocates for policies that promote economic growth, entrepreneurship, and lower taxes. While the Liberal Party is broadly liberal in its economic policies, it also incorporates conservative elements, particularly in social and cultural matters. This includes support for traditional family values, law and order, and national security.

The Australian Liberal Party was founded in 1944 with the aim of bringing together anti-Labor forces and providing a more cohesive alternative to the ALP. During Prime Minister Sir Robert Menzies' era, the Liberal Party pursued economic liberalism and anti-communist policies. After the 1975 federal election, the government implemented economic liberalisation policies. The Australian Liberal Party has traditionally espoused principles aligned with conservative and liberal values. In contemporary Australian political culture, the Coalition (Liberal and National parties) is considered centre-right.

According to Liberal education policy, the party is committed to needs-based schools funding. During Liberal party governments, funding for the non-government sector has increased.

Other Minor Parties

The Nationals: The Nationals primarily represent rural and regional interests, advocating for policies that support agriculture, primary industries, and rural communities. They often prioritise issues such as regional infrastructure, drought relief, and rural healthcare. Like the Liberal Party, The Nationals espouse conservative values on social issues, aligning with traditional family values and law and order policies.

Australian Greens: The Australian Greens promote environmental sustainability, ecological conservation, and renewable energy. They advocate for policies to address climate change, protect biodiversity, and transition to a low-carbon economy. The Greens are socially progressive, supporting progressive social policies such as marriage equality, gender equality, Indigenous rights, and multiculturalism. They often align with progressive movements on issues related to social justice and human rights.

Common Grounds for Labor and Liberals

Despite their differences, the ALP and the Liberal Party of Australia share some common ground on key policies, reflecting their mutual commitment to certain national interests. Both parties agree on the importance of maintaining a robust economy, although their approaches may differ. They support free trade agreements, recognising the benefits of international trade for Australia's economy. Both parties are committed to a strong national defence and security framework, including alliances like ANZUS and cooperation with global partners. Additionally, they share a commitment to addressing climate change, albeit with different strategies and targets, and they both recognise the need for infrastructure investment to support economic growth. Health care, another critical area, sees both parties supporting the Medicare system, though with varied approaches to funding and management.

In terms of school governance, both the ALP and the Liberal Party recognise the importance of providing quality education to all Australian students and support the principle of equitable access to education, regardless of socio-economic background. They agree on the necessity of maintaining high standards of teaching and learning, and both endorse the use of standardised testing to monitor student performance and educational outcomes.

Furthermore, both sides commit to consumer choice as a key driver of education excellence. Both parties support the autonomy of schools in making decisions that best suit their local communities while ensuring accountability through transparent reporting and governance frameworks. They also advocate for investment in school infrastructure to create conducive learning environments. These shared principles highlight their mutual commitment to fostering a robust and effective education system in Australia.

While their funding models differ, both parties emphasise the importance of quality education and skills development to ensure Australia remains competitive. Both parties are committed to policies aimed at closing the gap between Indigenous and non-Indigenous Australians in areas such as health, education, and employment. These commonalities illustrate a shared understanding of fundamental issues, even as they debate the best methods to achieve these goals.

Overall, education policies in Australia are determined through a combination of party platforms, leadership decisions, policy development processes, stakeholder consultation, and electoral dynamics. The specific approaches and priorities of political parties like Labor and Liberal may vary based on their respective ideologies, values, and electoral strategies.

Chapter 6

Exploring Key Concepts of School Finance & Governance

Introduction

This chapter introduces key concepts that are central to the themes of the book, helping readers to understand the materials more comprehensively. It presents concepts like education quality, adequacy, equity, equality, formula-based school funding, school choice, school autonomy, transparency, and accountability. These concepts emerge from different economic paradigms and evolving domestic and global educational policy directions.

Quality

Quality education encompasses holistic learner development, including knowledge acquisition, critical thinking, creativity, and socio-emotional well-being. It fosters an inclusive learning environment, ensuring equitable access for all students. Across economic paradigms, quality education holds significance. In Keynesian ideology, it is an investment in human capital for economic growth and social welfare, advocating for government intervention. Neoliberalism emphasises market-driven principles, equating quality education with choice and efficiency, promoting competition among schools. Post-neoliberalism recognises education as a human right, prioritising social equity and sustainability alongside economic development.

Regardless of economic ideology, quality education aligns with broader development goals, serving as a catalyst for poverty alleviation and social mobility. It is fundamental to upholding human rights, fostering tolerance, and intercultural understanding. Through inclusive education, nations can achieve sustainable development, harnessing its transformative power for a just and prosperous future.

Adequacy

With the increasing emphasis on educational quality and consequential outcomes, educators are advocating for reciprocal support and resources to meet these expectations. Likewise, parents believe increased funding can enhance educational outcomes for their children. These demands prompt policymakers to grapple with the question: What resources are necessary to ensure all students reach desired achievement levels?

The debate on school funding intertwines with the quest for improvement. While funding discussions in the US have often centred on equity—fairly distributing available funds—there's a growing focus on adequacy: determining how much is sufficient for educating a child.

Today, schools are urged to enhance the achievement of all students. However, when schools cite resource shortages, policymakers confront critical questions: What resources are required? What educational strategies and staffing are necessary for optimal performance? How can we address the needs of students with special requirements?

Adequacy-based funding models, addressing equity and equality, start with the base cost of education and adjust for student characteristics, school size, and type. They consider educational strategies, staffing, and specific student needs.

While adequate funding can enhance learning environments by providing qualified teachers, updated materials, and facilities, merely increasing funds does not guarantee improved quality. Efficiency and effectiveness in fund utilisation are crucial, considering various school needs and challenges.

Equity advocates call for even distribution of funds to address historical disparities, while adequacy proponents emphasise allocating resources based on specific student and school needs.

Equity and Equality

For policymakers, the first step in addressing student performance gaps is adjusting fiscal policy based on equity principles. According to Field, Kuczera, and Pont (2007), equity in schooling includes the dimensions of "fairness" and "inclusion." Fairness implies that personal and social circumstances are not obstacles in achieving educational potential, while inclusion refers to ensuring a minimum standard of education for all.

In the broader social context, equity refers to equality of opportunity, fairness, and social justice. In the context of educational finance, equity is a dual funding principle whose purpose is to 1) provide as much equality as possible in educational services, and 2) establish fairness in regards to the community sharing the tax burden for education (McGrath, 1993).

Equity is prone to two alternative and supplementary definitions: horizontal equity and vertical equity (Berne & Stiefel, 1984; Fazekas, 2012; Levacic, 2008).

Horizontal Equity

Horizontal equity emphasises treating similar individuals or entities in a similar manner. In the context of school finance, horizontal equity involves providing equal resources or funding to schools or students with similar needs or characteristics. This means that schools with similar student populations and educational challenges receive comparable levels of support. The goal of horizontal equity is to avoid unjustifiable disparities in resource allocation among schools or students who share similar characteristics.

Horizontal equity refers to funds allocated equally among schools that share certain characteristics. This definition does not assume that all schools have comparable needs; rather, it refers to the philosophy of "equal treatment of equals." For example, general education spending provides an equal base for all students. Thus, horizontal equity could provide a valid criterion upon which to evaluate equality of general education funding (Berne & Stiefel, 1994, p. 406; Bandaranayake, 2011).

Vertical Equity

Vertical equity focuses on the fair distribution of resources based on the varying needs and characteristics of students or schools. In the context of school finance, vertical equity often involves allocating more resources to students or schools with greater educational needs. This could include factors such as socioeconomic status, English language proficiency, special education requirements, or other indicators of educational disadvantage. The goal of vertical equity is to ensure that all students have an equal opportunity to achieve educational success, regardless of their individual circumstances.

Vertical equity is the notion that students should be treated according to their different learning needs and characteristics. This is the principle of "unequal treatment of unequals." This also implies that "differently situated children should be treated differently" (Levacic, 2008). Vesely & Crampton (2004) accepted the notion that vertical equity is a more complex and difficult concept to operationalise. The concept of vertical equity stresses that if students have different educational needs, an equitable state funding system should provide different levels of funding to meet these needs (Rubenstein et al., 2000). Therefore, in order to apply the vertical equity concept, one has to identify the relevant "differences in learning needs," which are typically defined in terms of educational input needs to achieve a defined level of performance (Berne & Stiefel, 1999).

Although the concepts of vertical and horizontal equity are fairly straightforward, constructing valid measures of each has been a complex task. In practice, education policymakers strive to strike a balance between vertical and horizontal equity, recognising that both are important for creating a fair and effective educational system. The goal is to allocate resources in a way that addresses individual needs while also promoting fairness and consistency across similar educational contexts (Bandaranayake, 2011).

Formula-Based Funding

A formula-based school funding system is a method of allocating financial resources to schools using a predetermined formula that takes various factors (adequacy, equity, equality, etc.) into account. The goal is to distribute funds in a fair, transparent, and consistent manner, reflecting the specific needs and characteristics of each school. This approach aims to promote equity in educational opportunities and outcomes. As outlined elsewhere, the Schooling Resource Standards at the commonwealth level and the Student Resource Package at the state level in Victoria are such formula-based school funding systems.

There is a range of principles and methods typically associated with a formula-based school funding system, which are based on school funding models for schools in Victoria:

- Per Student Funding Formula: This provides a foundational amount of funding per student, forming the base. Additional funds may be allocated based on student characteristics or local cost-of-living factors.
- Weighted Student Formula: This assigns different weights to students based on specific characteristics, such as English language proficiency, special education needs, or socioeconomic status. Schools receive additional funds for students with higher weights.
- Categorical Aid: This allocates funds for specific purposes, such as special education, bilingual education, or transportation. This method ensures targeted funding to address needs or programs.
- Equalisation Grants: These grants aim to reduce funding disparities between wealthier and less affluent districts, ensuring that all students have access to a similar level of resources.
- Performance-Based Funding: This ties a portion of funding to the achievement of specific performance

metrics. Schools meeting or exceeding these targets receive additional funds, fostering a focus on academic outcomes.

A well-designed formula-based school funding system considers the unique characteristics and needs of each school and aims to provide a fair and adequate level of resources to support educational success. It is important to continually evaluate and adjust the formula to address changing circumstances and educational priorities. Victoria has introduced a formula-based school funding system that has been in practice for over three decades (Bandaranayake, 2011).

Fiscal Federalism

School financing debates also intersect with broader discussions about fiscal federalism, which concerns the division of fiscal responsibilities and resources between different levels of government. Questions arise about the appropriate roles and responsibilities of federal, state, and local governments in funding education, as well as the mechanisms for revenue generation, redistribution, and accountability within the education system.

School Choice

School choice allows parents and students to select from various educational options beyond their assigned public school, including private schools, homeschooling, and online programs. In neoliberal economic frameworks, school choice aligns with market competition and consumer choice, advocating for education privatisation and market forces to drive improvement. Proponents argue this fosters efficiency and innovation, but critics warn of exacerbating inequalities and undermining public education.

In contrast, post-neoliberal paradigms view school choice through an equity lens, prioritising access to quality education regardless of socioeconomic status. This approach emphasises community engagement and collaborative solutions to address systemic inequities.

The core idea is to provide families with options that suit their needs. School choice initiatives introduce competition, including charter schools, vouchers, magnet schools, virtual schools, and homeschooling. Proponents believe this empowers parents, promotes innovation, and improves educational quality, while critics fear increased segregation and resource diversion from public schools.

Implementation varies globally, with policies tailored to local contexts and regulations. Advantages include diverse educational options, parental empowerment, and potential for innovation. However, disadvantages include exacerbating inequalities, resource diversion, and limited government oversight compromising standards.

Effective school choice policies strike a balance between autonomy and regulation, aligning with broader societal goals of equity, diversity, and quality education for all students.

School Autonomy

School autonomy pertains to schools' independence in managing internal affairs, curriculum, budget, and policies. Neoliberalism, an economic and political philosophy, prioritises limited government intervention, free-market capitalism, and individual entrepreneurship.

There are significant intersections between school autonomy and neoliberalism. Neoliberal policies advocate for decentralisation, devolving decision-making from central authorities to local levels, including schools. This is based on the belief that local actors, like administrators and parents, are better suited to make decisions tailored to their needs. Neoliberal education reforms, including school choice and competition, aim to improve outcomes by offering more choices and empowering schools to compete for enrollment. Charter schools, publicly funded with more autonomy, are seen as promoting innovation and efficiency, aligning with neoliberal principles.

While promoting autonomy, neoliberal education policies stress accountability, often measured through standardised testing. Schools are expected to deliver measurable outcomes in exchange for autonomy, leading to a shift from centralised to localised governance. Stakeholder engagement is encouraged to hold schools accountable.

Critics argue that excessive autonomy and market-oriented reforms may worsen inequalities, favouring schools with more resources and parental support. There are debates on the effectiveness of neoliberal policies, as emphasis on standardised testing and competition may narrow the curriculum and worsen educational inequalities.

Transparency and Accountability

Within neoliberal education funding policies, transparency and accountability play pivotal roles, reflecting the emphasis on market-oriented principles.

Transparency and accountability are fundamental aspects of neoliberal education funding. Decentralised funding mechanisms, like formula-based funding or voucher systems, are common in neoliberal policies. Transparent funding allocation entails clear and accessible criteria and formulas, ensuring fairness and equal opportunities for schools. Neoliberalism promotes school choice, where transparency is crucial in providing information about school performance and characteristics, empowering parents to make informed decisions and fostering healthy competition.

Performance metrics and accountability measures, such as standardised testing, are utilised to assess school effectiveness (e.g., NAPLAN, PISA). Transparent reporting of these metrics allows stakeholders to evaluate and compare school outcomes, creating a competitive environment where schools are accountable for their results. School autonomy is typically accompanied by accountability measures, requiring schools to innovate and improve while transparently reporting resource allocation and outcomes.

Despite these measures, critics highlight potential drawbacks of an overemphasis on standardised testing and market-driven competition, including curriculum narrowing and exacerbation of educational inequalities. Balancing transparency and accountability with broader educational goals remains a significant challenge in neoliberal education funding.

These concepts reflect various economic paradigms and evolving policy directions, each contributing to the ongoing dialogue about how best to provide equitable and high-quality education for all students.

Chapter 7

Distinctive Contextual Factors Affecting Australian Education

Introduction

Chapter seven delves into the distinctive contextual elements moulding the landscape of Australian education, serving as the driving forces behind its outcomes. It explores various factors such as Australia's abundant natural resources, stable political environment, colonial legacy, and the advantageous position of migrants, all playing pivotal roles in shaping educational policies and outcomes. Furthermore, it examines the enduring educational disparities faced by the First Nation, Aboriginal and Torres Strait Islander communities, presenting a complex interplay of challenges and opportunities in terms of school funding and governance strategies.

Natural Resources and Economic Prosperity

Australia is rich in natural resources. It has abundant energy resources, including coal, natural gas, and renewable energy sources such as solar, wind, and hydroelectric power. As one of the world's largest exporters of coal and liquefied natural gas (LNG), Australia's energy sector is a significant contributor to its economy. Additionally, Australia has vast agricultural lands that support the production of crops, livestock, and dairy products. Key agricultural products include wheat, barley, sugarcane, cotton, beef, lamb, and wool. The country also boasts rich marine resources and a diverse range of fish species, supporting both commercial and recreational fishing industries. Extensive forested areas, particularly in regions such as Tasmania and parts of New South Wales and Victoria, contribute to timber production, including hardwoods and softwoods. Furthermore, Australia has significant freshwater resources, although availability varies by region and is influenced by factors such as rainfall patterns and population density. The nation's vast landmass includes diverse ecosystems, ranging from tropical rainforests to arid deserts, home to unique flora and fauna found nowhere else in the world.

Australia enjoys a relatively stable economy and political landscape. The country has experienced consistent economic growth over the years, with its GDP growth rate hovering around 2-3% annually. Historically, Australia has maintained low unemployment rates compared to many other developed nations. Its economy is well-diversified, with significant contributions from sectors such as mining, agriculture, manufacturing, services (including finance, tourism, and education), and technology.

Australia is a stable democracy with a robust system of governance, characterised by regular free and fair elections, adherence to the rule of law, and respect for democratic institutions. Political transitions in Australia typically occur smoothly and peacefully, with power shifting between major political parties through democratic elections. Strong and independent institutions, including the judiciary, central bank (Reserve Bank of Australia), regulatory bodies, and public service agencies, contribute to political stability and good governance. Additionally, Australia is known for its social cohesion and multicultural society, with policies aimed at promoting diversity, inclusion, and social harmony. While political debates and differences exist, they are typically managed within the framework of democratic institutions and civil discourse.

Rich natural resources and economic prosperity in Australia provide ample financial resources for investment in education infrastructure, programs, and initiatives. This prosperity enables the Australian government to prioritise education funding, ensuring access to quality education for all citizens on an ongoing basis.

Political Stability

Australia's geographic location plays a significant role in global security. Situated in the Asia-Pacific region, which is increasingly becoming a focal point for global economic and strategic interests, Australia's location provides access to key sea lanes and trade routes, making it strategically important for maritime security and trade flows. Alliances and partnerships with countries such as the United States, New Zealand, and key Asian nations contribute to regional stability and security. These alliances enhance Australia's defence capabilities and provide mutual security assurances in the event of regional conflicts or crises.

Australians enjoy relatively high incomes compared to many other countries, with a median household income among the highest globally. The country has a strong labour market, with low unemployment rates and opportunities for employment in various sectors. Australia has a universal healthcare system known as Medicare, which provides affordable access to medical services for all residents. The country also boasts a high standard of healthcare infrastructure, medical research, and healthcare professionals, contributing to better health outcomes and quality of life. Additionally, Australia has a comprehensive social safety net, including welfare payments, pension schemes, and support services for vulnerable populations such as the elderly, disabled, and unemployed. These social services help alleviate poverty, reduce inequality, and ensure a basic standard of living for all citizens.

Political stability in Australia fosters a conducive environment for long-term education planning, policy development, and implementation.

Colonial Advantage

Australia's colonial advantage in adopting British institutions, governing systems, and legislation provided a robust foundation for developing a stable and effective government. The adoption of British common law offered Australia a well-established legal framework characterised by case law and judicial precedents. This comprehensive legal system, familiar to settlers and administrators, reduced the time and effort needed to establish a functional judicial system from scratch. Moreover, the British emphasis on the rule of law ensured that all individuals and institutions, including the government, were subject to the law, creating a fair and predictable legal environment essential for economic development and social stability.

The political and administrative systems in Australia benefited significantly from British influences, particularly through the adoption of the Westminster system of parliamentary democracy. This system, with its focus on representative democracy, responsible government, and the separation of powers, provided a tested and functional model of governance, ensuring political stability and accountability. Additionally, Australia inherited the British tradition of a professional and non-partisan civil service, which contributed to the efficient administration of government policies and services. This professional bureaucracy played a crucial role in effectively implementing laws and regulations across the vast and sparsely populated country.

Economic development in Australia was also greatly facilitated by following British economic practices. The establishment of economic institutions based on British models, including property rights, contract law, and market regulation, encouraged trade and investment. This framework supported economic activities both domestically and internationally, fostering growth and development. Furthermore, the introduction of banking and financial institutions modelled after British systems provided the necessary financial infrastructure for economic expansion and industrialisation, including a stable currency system, commercial banking, and financial markets.

The social and cultural influence of British institutions in Australia extended to the establishment of educational institutions and public services, which were crucial for social development. The introduction of a public education system based on British models helped improve literacy and education levels, supporting economic and social progress. Shared British cultural and social values provided a sense of identity and cohesion among settlers, helping to unify diverse communities and facilitate the integration of various social groups into a cohesive society. While British systems provided a strong foundation, they were also adapted to suit Australia's unique context, including its geography, demographics, and indigenous populations. This adaptability ensured that the institutions remained relevant and effective in addressing local needs and challenges.

Migrant Advantage

Australian migration policies and initiatives following the Second World War, especially those introduced in the early 1970s, have played a crucial role in enhancing and sustaining Australia's esteemed educational standing and skilled workforce. The nation's migration trajectory is increasingly focused on skilled migrants, recognised for their role in driving competitive advantage, innovation, and economic prosperity.

Initially settled by British convicts and overseers in 1788, Australia witnessed a significant influx of convicts, who eventually transitioned into free settlers and contributed to colonial development. The discovery of gold in the 1850s further catalysed immigration, attracting waves of migrants from Europe and China, bolstering population growth and economic expansion. However, post-federation in 1901, the implementation of the "White Australia" policy sought to restrict non-European immigration, albeit with exceptions for European immigrants, a policy gradually dismantled post-World War II. Subsequently, Australia initiated ambitious immigration programs to address labour shortages, particularly welcoming displaced persons and refugees from Europe.

The official end of the White Australia Policy in 1973 marked a pivotal shift towards a more inclusive and multicultural Australia, facilitating increased immigration from Asia and other non-European regions. In contemporary times, Australia's immigration landscape encompasses various programs, including skilled migration, family reunion, humanitarian and refugee programs, temporary visas, and the Global Talent Program. Particularly for migrants from Asia, drawn to Australia for educational opportunities and improved quality of life, educational aspirations are central, driven by personal growth, career advancement, and a better future.

Recent data suggests that high achievers in Australia do include individuals from language backgrounds other than English. While English-speaking students still make up a significant portion of high achievers, there is evidence to suggest that students from non-English language backgrounds are also well-represented among high achievers (ACER, 2019).

Indigenous Disadvantage

The plight of Indigenous Australians, particularly First Nations peoples, remains a deeply urgent political concern in Australia. Centuries of systemic marginalisation, land dispossession, cultural erasure, and socioeconomic disparities have profoundly impacted Aboriginal and Torres Strait Islander communities. Despite efforts towards reconciliation and acknowledgment of historical injustices, significant challenges persist in healthcare, education, housing, and justice, prompting ongoing debates and calls for substantive action and reform.

Understanding the demographic makeup of both Aboriginal and non-Aboriginal populations is crucial in addressing these disparities. Aboriginal and Torres Strait Islander peoples, with a heritage spanning over 65,000 years, comprise approximately 3.3% of the Australian population, while the non-Aboriginal population constitutes the majority at around 24.5 million.

Indigenous disadvantage in Australia spans various socioeconomic indicators, with Indigenous Australians typically experiencing poorer outcomes than their non-Indigenous counterparts. Despite some progress, significant disparities persist in health, education, employment, housing, and justice. From lower life expectancy and educational attainment to higher rates of unemployment, poverty, overcrowded housing, and overrepresentation in the criminal justice system, Indigenous Australians face complex challenges rooted in historical, social, economic, and political factors. Addressing these disparities requires comprehensive and targeted approaches that prioritise Indigenous voices, foster self-determination, and address structural inequalities across all sectors of society.

The Closing the Gap strategy in Australia aims to address these significant disparities. Launched in 2008, the strategy sets specific targets to improve outcomes for Indigenous Australians by 2031. These targets include closing the gap in life expectancy, halving the gap in child mortality rates, ensuring access to early childhood education, improving literacy and numeracy rates, increasing employment opportunities, and reducing incarceration rates. The strategy involves collaboration between the Australian government, Indigenous communities, and various stakeholders to implement policies and initiatives aimed at achieving these targets and improving the overall well-being of Indigenous Australians

Part II

Historical Outlook:
Evolution of Federal & State School Funding Policies

Chapter 8

Evolution of School Financing & Governance Policies in the State of Victoria

Introduction

In Chapter eight, Victoria's groundbreaking advancements in school governance and the implementation of formula-based funding reforms are examined. These initiatives seem to be primarily rooted in neoliberal economic principles.

School Financing Prior to the 1990s

Since the creation of the Department of Education in Victoria in 1872, the education administration was a centralised and growing bureaucracy involved in many decisions. Before the early 1990s, government schools were provided with resources that were administered and allocated entirely by the central bureaucracy. A large central bureaucracy managed all the affairs of schools and teachers. Teacher allocation to schools was based on historical traditions, which contained significant anomalies and inadequacies, failed to adequately consider the needs of individual schools, and had little educational validity.

The central bureaucracy had absolute control over the personnel and financial resources of schools. It was involved in the recruitment of teachers, their appointments, promotions, and transfers. Even all short- and long-term leave was controlled by the centre, as was the appointment of relief teachers. Teacher records and service histories, retirement, resignations, qualification assessment, teacher welfare, and teacher housing were all centrally managed.

Even school utility bills were paid centrally, and countless grants were administered by the department. Various grants for school-specific programs, facilities, equipment, and operations were managed centrally. This model provided tight central control and created a huge central workforce. Resources and policy decisions were made far from the local educational context of the school level.

Victorian principals have long argued that they could not be held responsible for the educational outcomes if they had no control over how the resources were allocated. An effective education system is one where schools are given the resources and flexibility to determine how best to meet the needs of their students (Hinz, 2010).

Victorian Reforms of Education Devolution

Victoria's education devolution reforms in the 1990s, under the Schools of the Future (SOFT) initiative, have been labelled as the most radical education reforms in the last century and had far-reaching effects beyond the boundaries of Victoria. The reforms had profound ramifications beyond Victorian borders, influencing other Australian governments and the evolution of conceptual frameworks for school funding and accountability (Hinz, 2010).

Schools of the Future reforms comprised three core elements: increased operating autonomy for government schools (devolving funding and hiring decisions), the introduction of a curriculum and standards across all schools, and increased accountability through state-wide assessment and reporting (Hayward, 1995).

Schools of the Future reforms were conceived by Don Hayward, the Liberal Party Minister for Education in Victoria, influenced by several popular school management concepts of the day (e.g., 'self-managing schools' by Caldwell & Spinks, 1988). He believed that quality outcomes of schooling could only be assured when decision-making occurred at the school level. He concluded that there was a crisis in education in Victoria, marked by declining confidence in the state public education system and government management, due in part to economic recession, a state budget deficit, higher parental and community expectations of schooling, and the power of teacher unions to block policies. He wanted to dismantle the system, reducing the power of unions (Campbell & Proctor, 2014; Hinz, 2010).

Don Hayward wanted government schools to become autonomous and independent providers. He championed greater autonomy and decision-making authority for individual schools, supporting the decentralisation of school governance, empowering school principals and councils to have more control over budgeting, staffing, and curriculum decisions. His policy included a substantial reduction of the size and functions of the department, the transfer of funding and school management responsibilities to individual schools, in accordance with the charter developed by the school councils and approved by the State Government, and authority for the principals to hire and fire and reward the teaching staff (Hayward, 1990; 1998). Despite the radical nature of the reforms, they were accommodated within the existing legislative framework.

Hayward was committed to promoting equity and inclusion in education. He advocated for policies and programs aimed at reducing educational disparities and supporting students from disadvantaged backgrounds, including initiatives to provide additional resources and support for schools in low-income areas.

School Global Budget

The significant change following SOFT was the new funding approach, which devolved the financial management responsibility to schools. The new funding allocation to individual schools was named the 'School Global Budget'. This comprised the total funds allocated to a school to implement the school charter, workforce planning, and full staff flexibility arrangements. This was the first time schools were able to match their resource allocation to their individual needs and goals (DET, 2013i).

The School Global Budget (SGB) revolutionised the funding and expenditure practices in Victoria. The two important practical elements of the Budget were credit and cash. Prior to 1994, all teachers were paid from the central payroll. The solution was to allocate salary-related funding for teachers and non-teaching staff to schools in the form of a credit budget. Schools were provided with a cash budget for expenses paid locally, such as cleaning, utilities, maintenance, class materials, professional development, and casual relief teaching. Schools were given the flexibility to transfer credit budget into cash and vice versa, according to their particular requirements. Under this model, schools managed their entire budget, but the Central Personnel Unit effectively operated as an outsourced payroll service.

During the transition period, there were issues of charging the global budget to the existing staff in schools. Some schools maintained experienced and expensive teachers, and therefore, if the school were to maintain the staff from the GSB, they could face a deficit. On the other hand, schools staffed with low-cost staffing profiles could have excess funds. Some schools had a curriculum imbalance with excess English and Arts teachers, and it was difficult to fill positions for math and science teachers. The solution was to use an average salary rate for budgeting purposes. Furthermore, during the transition period, schools were advised to indicate any excess teachers and allow them to charge their excess teachers outside the SGB for a period until they were redeployed. All schools were granted Full Staffing Flexibility by the end of 1996. The excess teacher procedures were maintained, but marked reductions were achieved through collaborative redeployment arrangements between schools and the central office.

The Global Budget Structure

The SGB was made up of six funding elements, each comprising a range of funding formulae, which applied to schools depending on their type, enrollment, size, location, and special equity factors. The elements included:

- Core funding: Approximately 80 percent of each school's Global Budget, including funding for classroom teachers, administrative and support staff, payroll tax, professional development, casual relief teachers, contract cleaning, maintenance, and utilities.

- Program for disabilities and impairments: Introduced a six-level index for all new students while retaining the current funding for existing students.
- Students with special learning needs: Focused on students with literacy problems contributed by personal circumstances, with a key funding component based on a weighted index using measures such as students receiving Education Maintenance Allowance (EMA), Koorie students, Languages Other Than English (LOTE), family status, and occupational status.
- Non-English-Speaking Background: Based on a seven-level composite index reflecting recent arrivals and previous relativities within English as a Second Language.
- Rurality and isolation: All schools in localities with up to 1,000 people were classified as rural schools and provided per capita allowances depending on their size.
- Priority programs: Identified non-mainstream funding for specific schools or groups, including programs such as music, sports, physical education (PE), and arts education in rural areas.

Since the implementation of the SGB, several changes have been made to improve historical inequalities and better focus the allocation of resources on individual student needs. These changes were supported by research and consultation with educational stakeholders.

The School Global Budget was the first major leap toward funding based on students and their learning characteristics. The new SGB started to shift the focus from providing inputs to providing resources, aiming to improve outcomes (DET, 2013i).

However, the new SGB was not without deficiencies in both structure and operation. For example, the funding did not fully reflect the relative importance of the early (foundation) years of schooling; funding levels were not based on the actual costs of teaching and did not accurately reflect the different costs associated with different stages of schooling; funding for teacher salaries — which was the largest component of the school global budget — did not address the inequality that average salaries were not evenly distributed across all schools.

SGB had the largest impact on popular or well-located schools with stable staff profiles concentrated toward the top of the incremental pay range or with relatively top-heavy leadership structures. These schools were required to develop workforce management strategies to manage their profiles within the budget over time.

Schools with salary costs much higher than the state-wide average were compensated with a supplement called Salary Profile Factor Funding. When an individual school's staff costs exceeded the state-wide benchmark, supplementary funding was provided. This supplementation was contentious because it was viewed as being inequitable and continuing to prop up expensive schools. It was seen as a flaw in the Global School Budget model, not consistent with the philosophy and principles of autonomy. It was subsequently removed in 2003 (DET, 2013i).

Student Resource Package (SRP)

Following the experience of the SOFT program and the School Global Budget, the Victorian Government, in 2003, initiated the development of a student-focused resource allocation model for schools based on the stages of schooling and benchmarks of equity. The model was subsequently titled the Student Resource Package. The name change was expected to emphasise the shift from a teacher-focused budget to a student-focused package. This SRP is still in operation with continuous improvements.

In 2003, the government developed a policy initiative – a Blueprint for Government Schools, which demanded a simpler, transparent, equitable funding model for improving educational outcomes. The initiative set a target of 90 percent of students successfully completing year 12 or its equivalent by 2010. A sound funding model was imperative. With the assistance of experts, empirical evidence was sought about the actual costs of funding efficient and effective Victorian schools, taking into account their local circumstances. This data was necessary to redesign credibility and gain acceptance for the new model from the community. There is a strong correlation between school effectiveness and the socioeconomic composition.

This package has been continuously improved from 2005 to date. The new and current funding system is explained in detail in Chapter 11.

Chapter 9

Evolution of Federal Government's Interventions in School Funding

Introduction

This chapter traces the historical trajectory of the Commonwealth Government's growing influence in school financing, highlighting pivotal milestones such as the Gonski proposals, the Australian Education Act 2013, Alice Springs (Mparntwe) Education Declaration, National Cabinet arrangements, and Education Regulations in 2023. It explores the journey leading to the introduction of shaping the landscape of education funding in Australia.

Power Dynamics Between State and Federal Governments

The establishment of the Commonwealth of Australia in 1901 united six former British colonies into a new nation, initiating shared governance responsibilities between the federal government and the states across various policy domains. Education emerged as a significant focal point, particularly concerning the principle of secularism within Australian education.

Australia contends with vertical and horizontal fiscal imbalances within its federation, stemming from the uneven distribution of fiscal responsibilities and resources between the federal government and the state and territory governments. Vertical fiscal imbalance arises from the federal government's dominance in revenue collection, juxtaposed with states' substantial expenditure obligations, notably in delivering critical public services like health, education, and infrastructure.

Horizontal fiscal imbalance reflects the differing revenue-raising capacities among states and territories due to economic variations and population disparities, leading to unequal funding capabilities. Addressing fiscal imbalances often involves mechanisms such as federal grants and revenue-sharing arrangements to redistribute funds and mitigate disparities, yet achieving equilibrium remains a complex challenge.

The Australian Constitution, Section 116, explicitly safeguards religious freedom, underpinning the notion of secular education in public schools. Historical debates in the early 20th century underscored tensions between the Commonwealth and state governments regarding funding for denominational schools versus a secular educational approach.

Substantial education funding reforms transpired in the 1960s and 1970s, notably with the Karmel Report of 1973 advocating for a needs-based funding model to tackle disparities. The subsequent Education Act 2013 reflects contemporary efforts, delineating funding frameworks for both government and non-government schools while emphasising needs-based funding principles to address educational inequities and ensure comprehensive quality education.

Commonwealth Authority in School Funding

The establishment of the Council of Australian Governments (COAG) in 1992 marked a significant step in coordinating government activities between the federal and state or territorial governments, including matters pertaining to education. Subsequent agreements, such as the Hobart Declaration on Schooling in 1989 and the Melbourne Declaration on Education Goals for Young Australians in 2008, underscored the growing trend towards national cooperation in education policy formulation and implementation. COAG played a central role in negotiating and implementing funding arrangements for education, facilitating the distribution of federal funding to states and territories.

Federal and State Financial Relations

The National Education Agreement (NEA), introduced in 2009, stands as one of the pivotal agreements between the Commonwealth and state governments, outlining funding allocations and accountability measures for education. Specific purpose payments (SPPs) under the NEA, including the National Schools Specific Purpose Payments (NSSPP), allocate funding to government and non-government schools, facilitating recurrent and capital funding based on measures of need.

Additional funding for schools is provided through special purpose National Partnerships (NPs), which vary in structure and conditions. These partnerships, such as the Digital

Education Revolution and Empowering Local Schools initiatives, aim to support schools in implementing system-wide reforms and meeting the diverse needs of students.

Gonski Review of Australian School Funding

In April 2010, then-Prime Minister Julia Gillard announced the commencement of a Review of Funding for Schools, famously known as the Gonski Review. From the 1980s onward, slogans like the 'clever country' (Hawke, 1990) framed education as a matter of international competitiveness. In the twenty-first century, this focus was solidified by the triennial PISA assessments, which significantly influenced the Gonski Review in 2011.

This comprehensive review culminated in the release of its final report in February 2012, emphasising the urgent need for an equitable school funding system that would bridge the gap in educational outcomes stemming from socioeconomic disparities. It highlighted the necessity of increased government expenditure on both public and private schooling to halt Australia's decline in international rankings. The Gonski Review proposed a groundbreaking national needs-based and sector-blind school funding model as a remedy to current inequities.

At the heart of the Gonski Review's recommendations was the concept of a Schooling Resource Standard (SRS), designed to determine the level of recurrent funding for all students. The SRS encompassed a per-student amount, differentiated for primary and secondary school students, alongside additional loadings for various sources of disadvantage, including socioeconomic background, disability, English language proficiency, indigeneity, and school size and location. Drawing on the resources utilised by high-achieving schools, as identified through the National Assessment Program — Literacy and Numeracy (NAPLAN), the SRS amounts were to be annually indexed to ensure relevance.

The review recommended a minimum public contribution per student for non-government schools, set between 20 percent and 25 percent of the SRS, excluding loadings, with loadings for disadvantage applicable to all eligible students regardless of the school attended.

Subsequently, the Australian Education Act 2013, introduced by the preceding Labor Government, embraced the Gonski model and its funding commitments, ushering in a new era for education in the nation. This pivotal legislation aimed to realign education funding in accordance with the principles outlined in the Gonski Review. Moreover, the imperative for intergovernmental cooperation was underscored by the "vertical fiscal imbalance," wherein the Commonwealth holds the lion's share of tax revenue-raising capabilities, while the states wield significant legislative powers in critical policy domains. Addressing policy imperatives necessitates substantial revenue transfers from the Commonwealth to the states, often entailing intricate negotiation and intergovernmental agreements.

Alice Springs (Mparntwe) Agreement

The Ministers of the Commonwealth and State/Territories met in Alice Springs in December 2019 and made the Alice Springs (Mparntwe) Education Declaration. This is a significant document that outlines the vision for education in Australia and the commitment to improving educational outcomes for young Australians. It builds upon past declarations from Hobart, Adelaide, and Melbourne, reflecting a continuous journey of enhancing the education system over three decades. The Declaration focuses on two interconnected goals: promoting excellence and equity in the Australian education system and ensuring that all young Australians become confident and creative individuals, successful lifelong learners, and active and informed members of the community. This commitment to education aims to position young people to lead fulfilling, productive, and responsible lives, contributing to the nation's social and economic prosperity.

The Alice Springs (Mparntwe) Education Declaration sets out the following education targets:

- Promoting excellence and equity in the Australian education system.
- Ensuring that all young Australians become confident and creative individuals, successful lifelong learners, and active and informed members of the community.

These targets emphasise the importance of providing quality education to all young Australians, regardless of background or circumstances, to support their personal growth, academic success, and societal engagement.

From COAG to National Cabinet

The National Cabinet was formed, replacing COAG, in response to the COVID-19 pandemic in Australia and held its first meeting in March 2020. Unlike COAG, which primarily involved political leaders, the National Cabinet includes the Prime Minister, state and territory premiers, and chief ministers, as well as key ministerial representatives. The National Cabinet operates as a smaller, more streamlined decision-making body focused on urgent and coordinated responses to national challenges, particularly during times of crisis such as the pandemic. While the National Cabinet initially focused on the COVID-19 response, it has since expanded its role to address other national issues, including economic recovery, vaccination distribution, and climate change mitigation.

The National Cabinet operates on a collaborative and cooperative basis, with decisions made by consensus among its members. It aims to facilitate more agile and effective decision-making while maintaining a unified approach across jurisdictions. Overall, the shift from COAG to the National Cabinet reflects a move towards greater flexibility, efficiency, and responsiveness in intergovernmental cooperation, particularly in times of crisis. The National Cabinet model seeks to foster closer collaboration between the federal government and state and territory governments to address pressing national challenges and deliver better outcomes for all Australians.

Structural Elements for Federal Level School Funding

At least five structural components, aligned with the principles of the Australian Education Act 2013, are instrumental in implementing federal government school funding policies. They include the National School Resourcing Board, National Schools Reform Agreements, and Bilateral Agreements.

The National School Resourcing Board (NSRB)

The National School Resourcing Board (NSRB), instituted in 2017 as part of educational reforms following the Gonski Review, oversees the Commonwealth schools funding model to ensure transparency and equity in resource allocation. It advises the government on funding matters, including the formulation of the National School Resourcing Standard (NSRS), under the Australian Education Act 2013 and the Australian Education Regulations 2023, aiming to bolster educational outcomes for all students.

Figure 3: Federal Structural Elements

	Federal Legislation	Australian Education Act 2013; Australian Education Regulations 2023.
	National Oversight	National School Resourcing Board.
	National level	**National Schools Reform Agreement** between all States and the Federal Government
	State level	**Bilateral Agreements** between each individual state and the federal Government
	Local Level	Registered individual schools and school improvement plans

Reviews conducted by the NSRB under the Act and Regulations aim to install public confidence in the funding model, ensure compliance, utilise robust data and methodologies, and align funding usage with legislative provisions.

National School Reform Agreement (NSRA)

The National School Reform Agreement (NSRA) commenced on January 1, 2019. The NSRA represents a collaborative policy framework jointly established by the Australian government and states/territories to tackle educational challenges and priorities. Succeeding previous COAG agreements, it aims to enhance educational equity and accessibility across the nation.

Outlined within the NSRA are national objectives concentrating on student achievement, teacher quality, and school leadership. Additionally, it includes funding arrangements aimed at facilitating educational reforms and improvements in school outcomes. The agreement emphasises collaborative governance, stakeholder engagement, and regional flexibility in policy implementation, advocating for evidence-based strategies aligned with national standards while promoting innovation in educational delivery. The next NSRA will commence in 2025.

Bilateral Agreements

Under paragraph 22(2)(b) of the Australian Education Act 2013, states and territories must establish Bilateral Agreements with the Commonwealth to improve student outcomes. These agreements are collaborative arrangements between states/territories and the federal government, tailored to each region's needs. They outline actions to enhance education quality and equity, covering areas like curriculum development, teacher training, and support for disadvantaged students.

Negotiations involve extensive consultation with education departments, schools, parents, and communities to establish clear goals. Bilateral agreements address various student cohorts. Once finalised, they guide federal funding allocation and are periodically reviewed to align with evolving educational priorities and track progress.

These structural components, aligned with the principles of the Australian Education Act 2013, are instrumental in implementing federal government school funding policies.

Part III

Methods of Funding:
Federal & Victorian School Funding Methods

Chapter 10

Federal Funding Methods to Government and Non-Government Schools

Introduction

Chapter ten introduces federal funding methods for government and non-government schools, aligned with the principles of the Australian Education Act 2013. It explores the School Resource Standard and various funding instruments, including recurrent and capital funding, along with accountability mechanisms to ensure policy effectiveness.

Schooling Resource Standard (SRS)

The Schooling Resource Standard (SRS) acts as an approximation of the overall public funding necessary for a school to effectively meet its students' educational requirements. Consisting of a foundational amount supplemented by up to six loadings based on needs (Student-based and School-based), the SRS is recalculated annually for each school by the Department of Education. This computation incorporates both the base amount and the loadings designated for the school, following formulas outlined in the Australian Education Act 2013. Additionally, the SRS sees yearly adjustments through the SRS indexation factor. As the cornerstone of the Commonwealth's ongoing funding distributions, the SRS outlines funding guidelines, with the Commonwealth funding a minimum of 20 percent for each government school's SRS and 80 percent for each non-government school's SRS, starting in 2024. Furthermore, the SRS framework is integral to the National School Reform Agreement, outlining the financial commitments from state and territory governments to schools.

SRS Base Amount

The SRS base amount is the fundamental element of the Schooling Resource Standard (SRS), representing the core funding allocated to meet the essential educational needs of students in a school. It forms the basis for determining the total public funding necessary to ensure quality education delivery. Calculating the SRS base amount involves multiplying the school's enrollment for the year by the designated SRS funding amount. However, for most non-government schools, the SRS base amount is adjusted based on the school's Capacity to Contribute (CTC).

SRS Loadings

The SRS loadings provide additional funding for student priority cohorts and disadvantaged schools. A school's SRS can include up to four student-based loadings and two school-based loadings. Loadings are not affected by capacity to contribute. A student may attract funding under more than one loading. The Department calculates the loadings for each school each year.

Figure 4: Federal Methods of Funds Allocation

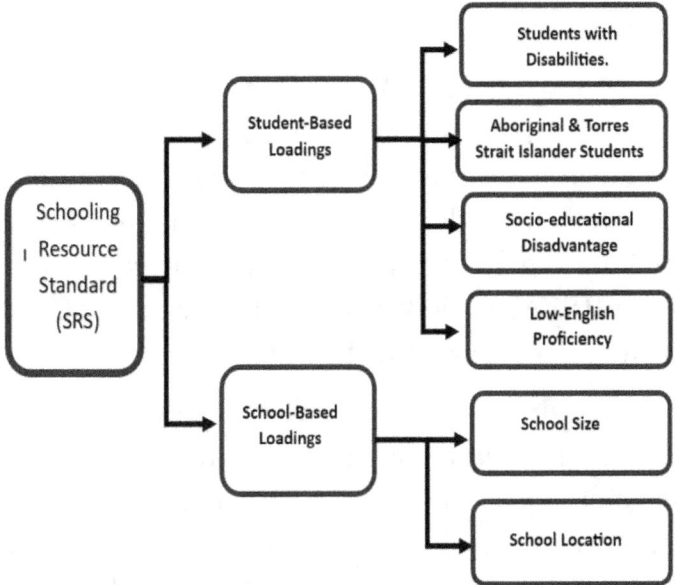

Student-Based Loadings

Students with Disability Loading: This allocation offers supplementary funding, alongside the SRS base amount, for students with disabilities. The amount allocated to a school depends on the number of students requiring additional assistance in the classroom to facilitate their full participation in school activities and the level of support needed. The calculation for this allocation utilises data reported in the Nationally Consistent Collection of Data on School Students with Disability (NCCD).

Aboriginal and Torres Strait Islander Loading: This allocation offers additional funding for each Aboriginal and Torres Strait Islander student. The amount of additional funding per student increases in correlation with the proportion of First Nations students enrolled in the school. If there is one First Nations student in the school, the allocation amounts to 20 percent of the SRS funding. This percentage escalates as the proportion of First Nations students in the school increases.

Socio-Educational Disadvantage Loading: This allocation offers supplementary funding for each student from a socio-educationally disadvantaged background. The amount allocated is determined by the percentage of students situated in the lowest two quartiles of socio-educational advantage (SEA), as developed by the Australian Curriculum, Assessment and Reporting Authority (ACARA).

Low English Language Proficiency Loading: This allocation offers supplementary funding for students from a language background other than English, where at least one parent has completed education only up to Year 9 or below. This group may encompass recently settled migrants and refugees. The allocation amounts to 10 percent of the SRS funding amount.

School-Based Loadings

School Size Loading: This allocation offers additional funding for medium, small, and very small schools, acknowledging that smaller schools cannot attain the same economies of scale as larger institutions. Primary schools with up to 300 students and secondary schools with up to 700 students qualify for the size allocation.

School Location Loading: This allocation offers supplementary funding for schools situated in regional and remote areas, recognising the typically higher costs associated with educating students in these locations compared to city-based schools. The allocation is determined based on a school's Accessibility/Remoteness Index of Australia (ARIA) score.

Capital Funding

The Capital Grants Program (CGP) provides funding to assist non-government primary and secondary school communities in improving capital infrastructure where they otherwise may not have access to sufficient capital resources. The aims of the CGP encompass enhancing and maintaining school capital infrastructure, with a focus on catering to the educational needs of disadvantaged students, prioritising the refurbishment and enhancement of existing capital infrastructure, and aligning with the Commonwealth's broader schooling priorities and objectives.

Funding is allocated in accordance with the Australian Education Act 2013 and distributed to each sector through the respective Block Grant Authority. Capital grants serve as supplementary resources to those provided by state and territory governments, non-government school authorities, and school communities, which bear the responsibility for the provision and upkeep of non-government school facilities.

These grants are based on need, with priority given to disadvantaged school communities with the least capacity to raise funds. Most long-established Independent schools receive no capital grants from governments. The extent and quality of their facilities reflect the contributions from families, former students, and other donors.

Capacity to Contribute

Capacity to Contribute (CTC) serves to diminish the SRS base amount for most non-government schools, assessing the financial capability of parents and guardians relative to other non-government schools to contribute to the school's operational costs. The CTC reduction does not affect SRS loadings for government schools, special schools, special assistance schools, majority Aboriginal and Torres Strait Islander schools, and sole provider schools.

The extent of the CTC reduction hinges on the school's CTC score, recalculated annually by the Department. This reduction varies from 10 percent of the SRS base amount for non-government schools with the lowest capacity to contribute, escalating to 80 percent for those with the highest capacity. Specific CTC scores and corresponding percentages are delineated in section 54 of the Australian Education Act 2013.

Funding Recipients

Under the Act, Australian Government recurrent funding for schools is distributed to 'Approved Authorities'. Approved Authorities are legal entities approved by the Commonwealth Minister for Education to receive Australian Government recurrent funding for one or more schools. An approved authority for more than one school redistributes Commonwealth recurrent funding to its member schools using its own needs-based funding arrangement. All government schools belong to their state or territory approved system authority. Most Catholic and some independent schools also belong to an approved system authority.

Schools Funding Assurance Framework

The Schools Funding Assurance Framework provides ensures transparency and accountability. It helps the Australian Government Department of Education to manage risks associated with error, non-compliance, and fraud in relation to Australian Government funding for school education under the Australian Education Act 2013 and the Australian Education Regulation 2023.

With Australian Government recurrent school funding reaching unprecedented levels, there is heightened scrutiny on fund utilisation and questions regarding the correlation between funding increases and improved school outcomes. To address this, the department collaborates with state and territory governments and other agencies to establish a unified regulatory environment, fostering cooperative data sharing and reducing administrative burdens.

Key areas of focus include the prevention of error, non-compliance, and fraud by assisting Approved Authorities in maintaining compliance and conducting assurance activities to detect instances of non-compliance. The framework employs a risk-based approach to monitor compliance and outlines responses to instances where Approved Authorities fail to meet requirements.

Given the evolving legislative and policy landscape, such as the implementation of the Quality Schools package, the department emphasises the need for an adaptable assurance approach. The framework ensures confidence in funding usage alignment with legislative requirements and prepares for future changes in the educational landscape.

In practical terms, the framework ensures:

- Appropriation of Australian Government funding in accordance with Act and Regulation requirements.
- Support for Approved Authorities in achieving and maintaining compliance.
- Identification and resolution of instances of non-compliance.
- Prevention of undue compliance burden on Approved Authorities.

- Recognition and rectification of systemic compliance issues.

Encompassing all major funding streams for government and non-government Approved Authorities, including recurrent funding, capital grants, and other grants, the framework strives to ensure transparent, consistent, and needs-based funding allocation.

Chapter ten elucidates the federal funding methods for government and non-government schools in Australia, emphasising the principles of the Australian Education Act 2013. It discusses the School Resource Standard (SRS) and its components, including the base amount and various loadings to address specific educational needs. The chapter also outlines capital funding mechanisms and the Capacity to Contribute (CTC) model, ensuring equitable distribution of resources. Additionally, the Schools Funding Assurance Framework is highlighted as a critical tool for maintaining transparency and accountability in the allocation and utilisation of funds, ensuring compliance with legislative requirements and promoting confidence in the education system's financial management.

Chapter 11

State Government Funding Methods for Victorian Government Schools

Introduction

Chapter eleven delineates the Victorian government's funding procedures for government schools through the Student Resource Package (SRP), which employs a formula-based funding approach. It encompasses student-based allocations for fundamental and equity requirements, school-specific funding for infrastructure and initiatives, and targeted programs covering a range of focused endeavours. Beginning with an overview of federal and state funding streams, the chapter proceeds to detail the funding mechanisms tailored specifically for Victorian government schools.

Federal and State Funding Channels

The previous chapter described the Federal government funding methods to government and non-government schools. However, it is important to note that most of the federal funds to schools go through the departments of state governments. In addition, some funds go to non-government schools through block grants authorities. Figure... outlines the channels and categories of Federal and Victorian government funds distribution to both government and non-government schools.

Figure 5: Victorian school funding Framework

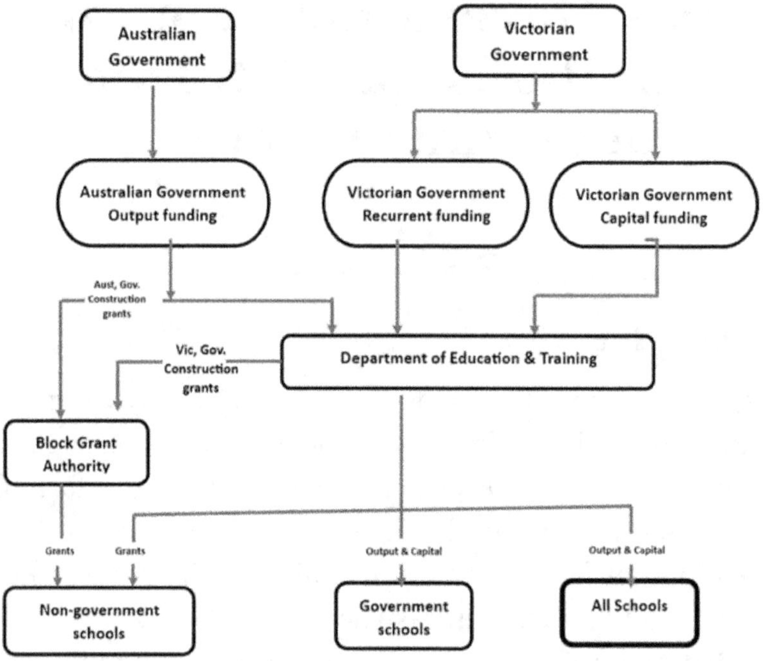

```
                    Australian                         Victorian
                    Government                         Government
                         │                    ┌────────────┴────────────┐
                         ▼                    ▼                         ▼
              Australian Government    Victorian Government     Victorian Government
                 Output funding          Recurrent funding         Capital funding
                    │                         │                         │
         Aust. Gov. │                         │                         │
         Construction                         │                         │
         grants  │  │                         │                         │
                 │  │        Vic. Gov.        │                         │
                 │  │      Construction       │                         │
                 │  │         grants ─────────┤                         │
                 │  │                         ▼                         │
                 │  │        Department of Education & Training         │
                 │  │                                                   │
                 ▼  ▼                                                   │
              Block Grant                                               │
               Authority                                                │
                 │   │                                                  │
             Grants  Grants        Output & Capital        Output & Capital
                 ▼   ▼                    ▼                         ▼
             Non-government           Government                All Schools
                schools                 schools
```

(Source: Victoria Parliamentary Budget Office.)

Funding to Victorian Government Schools

In Victoria, state government funds allocated to government and non-government schools are distributed through the Victorian Department of Education (DET).

Student Resource Package (SRP)

In Victoria, the Student Resource Package (SRP) is a key funding mechanism used by the Department of Education and Training to allocate resources to government schools. The SRP aims to ensure that each government school has the necessary funding to meet the diverse needs of its students and deliver quality education. The SRP encompasses funding for various components, including staffing, operational costs, student support services, and infrastructure maintenance. It considers factors such as student enrollment numbers, socio-economic status, and specific educational needs within each school community.

Credit and Cash Funding

In the context of Victorian government schools in Australia, SRP funding is provided through a combination of credit and cash components.

Credit Component: The credit component refers to the funding that schools receive based on a per-student allocation. This funding is intended to cover the general operating costs of the school, such as teacher salaries, utilities, maintenance, and administration. The per-student allocation may vary depending on factors such as the student's level of education (primary or secondary) and any additional needs they may have.

Cash Component: The cash component is additional funding provided to schools based on specific criteria or circumstances. It is usually allocated to address specific needs or priorities identified by the government. The cash component can be used for targeted initiatives, such as improving educational outcomes for disadvantaged students, implementing specific programs or projects, or investing in infrastructure upgrades.

The allocation of funding between the credit and cash components is to ensure that schools receive a base level of funding through the credit component while providing additional resources through the cash component to address specific educational needs and promote equity across schools.

SRP Funding Categories

The SRP has three main funding categories:

- Student-based funding
- School-based funding
- Targeted initiatives

Each category contains several subcategories.

Student-based Funding

Core student learning allocation and equity funding are the two primary types of student-based funding. Core student learning allocation funding is the main source of funding for schools, constituting around 90% of the total SRP provided to schools. It encompasses various expenses such as core teaching and learning, leadership, teaching support, professional development, relief teaching, payroll tax, and superannuation costs for the school.

Core Student Learning Allocation

The Core Student Learning Allocation is designed to recognise the differing costs associated with different levels of learning, different types and sizes of schools, and the additional costs imposed by rurality and isolation.

Student Per-Capita Funding: Student per capita funding constitutes 80 percent of resource allocation to schools, making it the primary category. The Core Student Allocation chiefly comprises per capita allocation for students from preparatory (Prep) to year 12 across all state schools.

Figure 6: State Methods of Funding Allocation

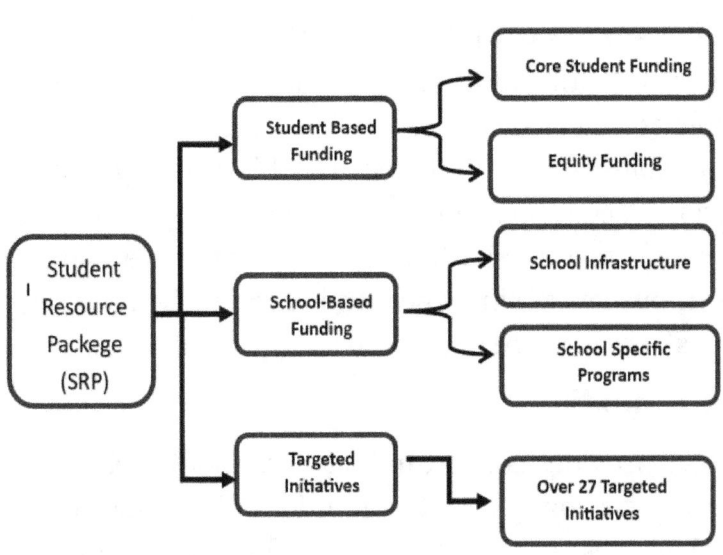

Allocations are determined based on research conducted in Victorian government schools, which identifies the costs associated with achieving successful educational outcomes across various levels and years of schooling, establishing relative weights between 1.0 and 1.33.

Enrolment-Linked Base: The Enrolment Linked Base (ELB) is designed to ensure that all schools, regardless of their size, receive adequate resources to function effectively. This flat base with a taper serves as a safety net for small schools with enrollments insufficient to generate viable funding. The taper also acknowledges the economies of scale achievable in larger schools through per student rates.

Small School Base: A Small School Base is allocated to primary schools with fewer than 80 students and secondary schools with fewer than 400 students. In primary schools, the base decreases as enrollments increase. In the case of multi-site primary schools, the base and taper are applied to each site individually.

Rural Size Adjustment: This funding allocation acknowledges the need for additional resources in small rural schools to ensure they can deliver high-quality education comparable to urban schools. Eligible primary, secondary, and combined schools located in non-metropolitan and non-provincial areas receive funding. Allocations are calculated at the campus level using a per student rate, divided into credit and cash components.

Equity Funding

The SRP provides equity funding where additional funding is required to compensate for additional learning needs. The specific types of equity funding include Equity (Social Disadvantage), Equity (Catch Up), Mobility, Programs for Students with Disabilities, and English as an Additional Language funding.

Equity (Social Disadvantage): Equity funding for Social Disadvantage offers individual support for students from disadvantaged backgrounds, with funding increasing according to the level of disadvantage within the school. Social disadvantage often puts students at a significant disadvantage compared to their peers upon entering the education system. Increased funding has been shown to improve educational outcomes, especially for these students.

Equity – Catch Up: Equity (Catch Up) funding aims to support students at risk of educational underachievement upon entering secondary school. Students who did not meet the national minimum standards in the National Assessment Program — Literacy and Numeracy (NAPLAN) in Year 5 (Reading) will each receive the Catch Up loading.

Mobility: Schools experiencing frequent student turnover for an extended duration qualify for mobility funding. This funding is intended to support schools in developing tailored programs to address the specific needs of mobile students. Eligible schools have a transient enrolment density equal to or exceeding 10 percent averaged over three years.

Students with Disabilities: The Program for Students with Disabilities (PSD) is a specialised supplementary funding initiative tailored for Victorian government schools. It allocates resources to schools catering to a specific group of students with disabilities, particularly those with high needs, to facilitate the delivery of tailored educational programs.

English as an Additional Language (EAL): The EAL program funding within the Student Resource Package (SRP) for primary and secondary schools primarily comprises EAL Index funding (Levels 1-5), allocated to schools meeting specific criteria. EAL funding is aimed at addressing language barriers, with allocations determined by the number of students from non-English-speaking backgrounds or those using a language other than English at home as their primary language.

School-Based Funding

Infrastructure Funding: This includes support for school facilities and encompasses various components such as contract cleaning, cross-infection prevention allowance, cleaning minimum allowance, grounds allowance, building area allowance, split-site/multi-site allowance, utilities, maintenance and minor works, annual contracts, and workers' compensation.

School-Specific Programs: Funding for "school-specific programs" is allocated to schools to address individual school needs and initiatives. This includes programs like the P12 Complexity Allowance, Location Index Funding, MARC/MACC Teachers, Science and Technology, Instrumental Music Programs, Bus Coordination, Country Area Program Grant, Alternative Settings Teachers, Ancillary Settings Teachers, Alternative programs — regional grants, Joint Community Program, and Designated Bilingual Programs.

Targeted Initiatives

Funding for targeted initiatives is one of three categories of funding provided by the SRP. The targeted initiatives component provides funding for programs with specific targeted criteria and/or defined lifespans. The SRP for 2024 lists 27 specific types of targeted initiatives, including Primary Welfare, Late Enrollment and Senior Secondary Re-engagement, Doctors in Secondary Schools — School Program Lead Funding, Respectful Relationships, Career Education Funding, Swimming in Schools, Head Start, National Student Wellbeing Program (NSWP), Middle Years Literacy & Numeracy Support (MYLNS) Initiative, Student Excellence Program Funding, and VCE Revision Lectures.

Chapter eleven details the Victorian government's Student Resource Package (SRP), a formula-based funding system. The SRP covers student-based core and equity needs, school-specific infrastructure, initiatives, and targeted programs, ensuring adequate resources for quality education based on socio-economic status and location.

Chapter 12

State Government Funding Methods to Victorian Non-Government Schools

Introduction

Chapter twelve outlines state government funding methods for non-government schools in Victoria. Funding encompasses direct allocations and program-based funding, categorised into two formulas: core funding, based on per capita funding adjusted for schooling stages and wealth, and need-based funding, considering factors like family background, disabilities, Indigenous status, and rurality. Additionally, there are program-based funding initiatives and capital funding programs.

State Funding to Non-Government Schools

The Victorian Minister for Education has a legislative responsibility for the education of all primary and secondary school students in Victoria, including those in non-government schools. The State Government provided project-based funding to non-government schools since 1967. Systematic funding to non-government schools commenced in 2006 and stemmed through three quadrennial agreements from 2006–2009, 2010–2013, and 2014–2017.

Victorian non-government schools must be registered and must operate on a not-for-profit basis to be eligible to receive Victorian Government funding. The Victorian Registration and Qualification Authority (VRQA) maintains a register of education and training providers, including non-government schools. From 2006, all registered non-government schools need to sign a funding and service agreement with the Victorian Government to access the state grant. Systematic schools will be bound by the funding and service agreement signed by their system authority.

Legislation to Determine Funding Amount and Accountability Requirements

The Education and Training Reform Amendment (Funding of Non-Government Schools) Act 2015 set a limit on the minimum amount of funds allocated to the non-government school sector. The legislation guarantees that non-government schools would receive at least 25 percent of the funding provided to government schools. The details of the new arrangements are contained in the Ministerial Order for funding to Catholic and independent schools (the details were not available at the time of this publication).

The legislation also established a School Policy and Funding Advisory Council to advise the Minister for Education about regulatory, policy, and funding issues affecting government and non-government schools. The Council consists of the Secretary for the Department of Education and Training (to be the Chairperson), a representative from the Catholic Education Commission, a representative from Independent School Victoria, and a representative from government schools.

The Council will provide advice to the Minister on regulatory, policy, and funding issues that affect government and non-government schools and include a focus on:

- Cross-sectoral reforms that will contribute to improved Victorian school education system outcomes;
- Funding, accountability, and reporting issues that affect government and non-government schools, including the development of funding agreements with non-government schools;
- Policy development that contributes to improved outcomes for specific cohorts (e.g., students with disabilities, Koorie students, students from low socio-economic backgrounds, and new arrivals);
- Regulatory issues with consideration given to advice provided by relevant statutory authorities;
- Commonwealth-State issues (e.g., National Partnerships and Commonwealth Government reviews and targeted programs);
- Maintaining high performance for all students in Victoria and enhancing collaboration between sectors.

The legislation also established accountability and reporting requirements for non-government schools. The changes empowered the Minister to place any reasonable conditions on funding provided and allowed the Minister to require a non-government school and/or its organising body to provide a report on the application of funding. The Minister is entitled to seek advice from the School Policy and Funding Advisory Council regarding these accountability reports.

The Current Funding System

The state government funding methods can be traced from the Victorian-Auditor General's report of 2016 and the Financial Assistance Model (FAM) that has been developed and modified since 2006.

Victorian-Auditor General's Report

The Victorian-Auditor General's report (2016) identifies and describes several categories: state recurrent grants, disability support grants, special purpose grants, facilitation and reward funding, and capital programs.

Financial Assistance Model (FAM)

Victorian government funding to non-government schools is based on the Financial Assistance Model (FAM) developed in 2006. FAM has been modified since then. FAM comprises two funding components: core funding provided on a per-capita basis, and needs-based funding, determined by the student and school characteristics profile, and funding for students with disabilities.

Core Funding: Core funding comprises a base level of per capita funding modified by stages of schooling relativities. The base level of funding for primary and secondary students is the minimum per capita level of funding allocated to schools under the FAM, which uses the Education Resources Index (ERI) for calculation. The ERI measures the capacity of a non-government school to generate its own income through fees, investments, fundraising, and donations compared to the standard level of resources. Stages of schooling relativities determine the year level per-capita rates.

Pursuing Equity

Figure 7: State Methods for Funds Allocation to Non-Government Schools

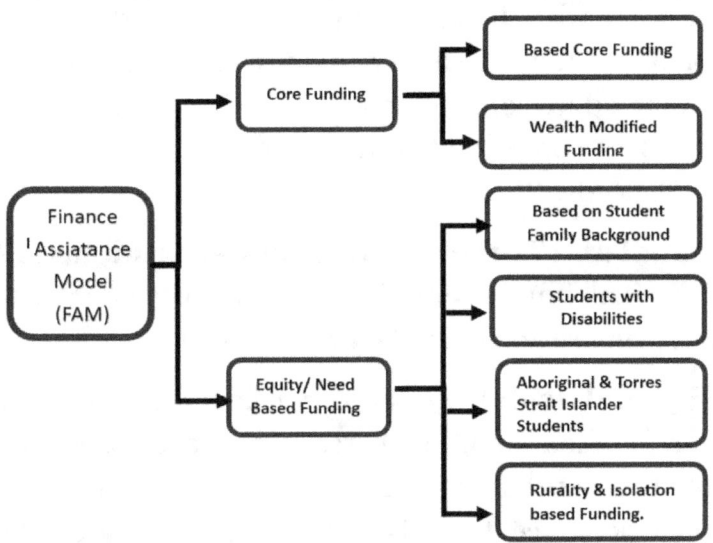

Wealth-Modified Funding: Core funding incorporates the wealth-modified element, which is based on an assessment of each school's capacity to support its students. Per-capita payments under the wealth-modified component are calculated by multiplying a base rate by an index based on the Commonwealth-designed Socio-Economic Status (SES) levels and incorporating the stages of schooling relativities.

Need-Based Funding: Four need-based factors are identified in calculating a school's need-based funding element — the student's family background, students with disabilities, Aboriginal and Torres Strait Islander students, and rurality.

Student Family Background: This entitlement is calculated based on the number of students enrolled at the school who are in receipt of the Educational Maintenance Allowance (EMA), which provides financial assistance to low-income families to help with the costs of essential educational items.

Students with Disabilities: These students have additional learning needs and require targeted support to reach their educational potential. FAM includes a stand-alone funding component to direct resources toward these additional needs.

Aboriginal and Torres Strait Islander Students: FAM has additional funding for this category of students, with different primary and secondary rates applied.

Rurality and Isolation: FAM considers that schools in rural areas face additional resource requirements. To calculate this entitlement, factors such as distance from the nearest regional centre, distance from the nearest large school, and distance from Melbourne are used.

Other State Funds Available to Non-Government Schools

Capital Grants for Non-Government Schools: Under the Capital Grants Program, non-government primary and secondary schools receive funding to enhance infrastructure in cases where capital resources are insufficient. This funding is allocated through the Australian Education Act 2013 and disbursed to each sector by the relevant Block Grant Authority.

Learning Support Tutor Initiative: Launched in 2021, the Tutor Learning Initiative (TLI) offers government and low-fee non-government schools funding to hire tutors for providing targeted small group learning assistance to students requiring additional support, primarily focusing on enhancing literacy and numeracy skills.

Conveyance Allowance Program: This program contributes to transportation costs for students attending government or non-government schools who travel via public transport, private vehicles, motorbikes, bicycles, or buses when the nearest school is not served by a free school bus provided under the School Bus Program.

Mental Health Support in Primary Schools: Participating schools receive funding to employ a Mental Health and Wellbeing Leader—a qualified teacher—to implement a comprehensive approach to mental health and wellbeing throughout the school community, encompassing students, staff, and families.

Respectful Relationships Program: Embedded within the Victorian Curriculum from foundation to year 12, the Respectful Relationships education aims to install a culture of respect and equality across the school community. This program supports schools and early childhood settings in promoting and modelling respect, positive attitudes, and behaviours while teaching students how to foster healthy relationships, resilience, and confidence.

National Student Wellbeing Program (NSWP): The NSWP offers pastoral care services and strategies to support the overall wellbeing of the school community, complementing the services provided by qualified specialists.

Swimming in Schools Initiative: Inclusive of both government and non-government schools, the Swimming in Schools initiative ensures that swimming and water safety education are integral components of the Victorian Curriculum (F-10). By Year 6, students are expected to demonstrate proficiency in the Victorian Water Safety Certificate (VWSC).

Accountability Reporting

In exchange for funding, the State Government mandates access to specific performance and resource data from non-government schools. This information is essential for the government to:

- Fulfill its responsibility in overseeing statewide education provision
- Monitor and comprehend school performance trends
- Ensure the efficiency and effectiveness of government funding
- Facilitate policy development and evaluation.

To alleviate the compliance burden on non-government schools, the state government only requests additional information beyond what is already provided to Commonwealth Government agencies. The state government endeavours to obtain this information directly from Commonwealth agencies whenever feasible.

Every school must furnish a school finance report by June 30th annually. This report is a certification provided by an auditor or accountant, verifying whether the funds disbursed under the funding agreement for the previous year have been utilised for their designated purpose. Additionally, the report outlines the financial activities of the school throughout the preceding calendar year, covering both income and expenditure. Compliance with this requirement is essential to ensure satisfaction from both the State Government and the Commonwealth Government.

Part IV

Structural Frame of Finance: School Finance Framework in Victoria

Chapter 13

Revenue Structure of Victorian Government Schools

Introduction

Chapter thirteen delves into the revenue framework of Victorian government schools, providing valuable perspectives on the array of funding sources available within the realm of school autonomy. This chapter is pivotal for comprehending how schools exercising operational independence handle their financial affairs. It encompasses an exploration of both state government and Commonwealth funding, in addition to other revenue streams including local fundraising, trading activities, student fees, curriculum contributions, donations, facility rentals, income from international students, international partnerships, and interest accrued from savings and investments.

Revenue in Victorian Government Schools

Cash Grants from SRP

As described under Chapter Six, fund allocations for schools in Victoria are nominated in credit and/or cash. The credit component contains allocations for staff salaries paid on the central payroll of the Department. That credit component is regarded as school revenue but not directly controlled by the schools. The cash component includes cash allocations for discretionary use by schools to meet expenses incurred locally. The cash component includes the Student Resource Package (SRP) student-based funding, school-based funding, and targeted initiatives. Cash and credit allocations to Victorian government schools include both state and Commonwealth government funding. Commonwealth funds are received by the State Government and put into one basket before allocating to government schools.

Commonwealth Grants

This category of Commonwealth grants is for specific purposes and is received directly by individual schools without channelling through the state Department of Education and Training. Examples include:

Commonwealth Capital Grants (for capital items)

- Commonwealth Government Grants (for specific programs)
- Outside School Hours Care Grants (operation of before and after school care programs)
- Grants for significant improvements in Aboriginal enrollments (cultural programs and relevant individual school programs)
- Early childhood development grants (kindergartens, pre-school centres, mental health)
- Maintenance grants for existing land and building assets
- Other specific grants such as primary school library grants

Schools may also receive grants from local governments for capital non-current assets and maintenance of existing land and building-type assets.

Funds from Local Fundraising Activities

Fundraising is a school council responsibility. These funds are for discretionary use by school councils, over and above the government funds to schools. The school council must approve the fundraising activity after estimating the revenue and expenditure and how the activity benefits the students. Fundraising activities range from school fairs, gala/carnivals, sausage sizzlers, raffles, musical shows, productions, and bingo sessions.

Donations

This category includes donations from businesses, groups, or individuals. Individual businesses can donate to the school for general purposes that are not tax-deductible.

Revenue from Trading Operations

School councils are entitled to conduct various trading operations as a school community service and as a fundraising activity. Typical activities include:

- Canteen operations
- Uniform sales
- New and second-hand book sales
- Before and after-hours school care

Each trading operation requires the approval of the school council. A profit and loss statement must be prepared at least annually for audit purposes. There must be ongoing monitoring of the school trading operations to ensure efficiency and effectiveness.

Outside School Hours Care

All payments received from parents related to an Outside School Hours Care (OSHC) program registered under the Commonwealth government. The revenue is taxable where the program is not registered under federal requirements.

International Student Fees

Some Victorian Government schools enrol international students who pay tuition fees. These fees contribute to the school's revenue and help support educational programs and services.

School Facilities Hire

With the approval of the school council, the school can hire out facilities such as school halls, equipment, playgrounds, and the like. The school council or the principal must monitor the actual performance against budget projections for the hire of facilities or equipment. All school facility hirers must carry their own public liability insurance.

Charities and Collections

Schools act as agents for the collection of funds used for receipting funds collected from local activities. These collections include monies collected for appeals (e.g., Royal Children's Hospital, Red Nose Day, Footy Colours Day) and book club or book fair collections.

Parents' Voluntary Contributions

Parent contributions come under curriculum contributions, extra-curricular activities, and other categories. Schools cannot refuse students instruction in the curriculum or disadvantage students based on financial contributions and payments not being made.

Curriculum Contributions: These include voluntary financial contributions for curriculum items and activities deemed necessary by the school. Parents can be invited to contribute to:

- General classroom materials and equipment (e.g., shared classroom stationery, paper, posters/charts, craft items, classroom libraries, readers)
- Subject-specific materials and equipment (e.g., materials for English, Mathematics, Language, Science, Art, Music, Technology, Food Technology, Health, and Physical Education)
- Provision and upkeep of school devices, peripherals, and ICT (e.g., devices owned by the school, class sets, device configuration, maintenance, and server/system costs)
- Photocopying and printing for students (e.g., printed learning resources)
- Curriculum activities (e.g., excursions, incursions, camps, whole-school carnivals, including transport and entry)
- Digital and online subscriptions for learning
- Assessments (e.g., online standardised testing)
- Supplementary classes within the school's swimming and water safety program and associated costs (attended by all students)
- Student planners/diaries

Extra-Curricular Items and Activities: These include items and activities that enhance or broaden the schooling experience of students and are above and beyond what the school provides for free to deliver the curriculum. These are provided on a user-pays basis (GST-free). Examples include sports teams, camps, music programs, and other activities.

Other Contributions: Voluntary financial contributions for non-curriculum items and activities related to the school's functions and objectives. Examples include:

- School buildings and grounds/library maintenance and enhancement
- School Building, Library, or Special School DGR accounts (these funds are approved by the ATO and are tax-deductible)
- Enhanced wellbeing support (e.g., wellbeing programs, school counsellors, mental health practitioners)
- Engaging staff through local payroll (e.g., groundskeepers, additional wellbeing, and learning support staff)
- Sports affiliation costs (e.g., School Sports Victoria affiliation)
- Student and parent communication tools
- Enhanced student support (e.g., learning support programs, tutoring, homework clubs)
- First aid and hygiene costs
- Lockers/locker maintenance

Other Locally Raised Funds

This includes all other funds received which are not government funds. They are used for receipting and include:

- Advertising by local businesses via newsletters and billboards
- Sponsorships
- Bursaries

- Insurance
- Graduations (not for students)

International Relationships

This category includes funds received to support international relationships and programs. Examples include funds received from external organisations or other countries to partake in or support exchanges, sister school arrangements, visits, programs, and activities.

Interest from Savings or Investment Accounts

The school council has the authority to hold surplus funds, not required immediately, to invest and generate interest revenue for the school. The school council must decide and approve the financial institution(s) in which to invest the funds. To minimise risk, schools should aim to limit their exposure to risky investments.

The High Yielding Investment Account (HYIA) was established by DET to assist schools with cash flow planning and to provide an attractive and competitive interest rate on surplus funds, while still retaining an 'at-call' status. Use of the HYIA simplifies the establishment of a school council's investment policy and eliminates the need for maintaining an investment register for that account.

Camps and Excursions

An excursion is an activity organised by a school during which students leave the school grounds to engage in educational activities (including camps and sports). Adventure activities are included in this definition (regardless of whether they occur outside the school grounds or not). A record must be kept of the revenue and expenditure for individual excursions. Any decision by the school to subsidise excursions must be approved by the school council.

Other Revenue

Other avenues for collecting revenue for individual schools include:

- Proceeds from the sale of class materials, such as furniture, equipment, and motor vehicles
- Sponsorship advertising by local businesses via newsletters and billboards
- Curriculum-related special events
- Debutante balls, school socials/formals
- School productions
- Math competitions, music competitions, and the like

Summary of Revenues Stated on My School Website

The My School website (http://www.myschool.edu.au/) provides a summary of financial information, both income, and expenditure, for each individual government and non-government school in Australia. This website is maintained by the Australian Curriculum Assessment and Reporting Authority (ACARA). On the website, once a school is selected by a reader, the first page outlines the school profile, which includes a brief section on the school's latest finances (e.g., total net recurrent income, per student net recurrent income, and total capital expenditure).

There are four recurrent income sources for each individual school as presented on the My School website:
- Australian Government Recurrent Funding: This figure includes income sourced from funding provided by the Australian government for recurrent purposes

such as employee salaries, overheads, goods and services, miscellaneous expenses, and travel.
- State/Territory Government Recurrent Funding: This figure includes income sourced from funding provided by State and Territory governments for recurrent purposes. In Victorian government schools, this item includes both cash and credit grants.
- Fees, Charges, and Parent Contributions: This figure represents the income received from parents for the delivery of education to students. For non-government schools, this figure represents school fees, and for government schools, it represents parent contributions explained in a previous section of this chapter.
- Other Private Sources: This figure shows income received from other sources such as donations, interest on bank accounts, profits from trading activities, and profits from the sale of assets. It includes some private income received for capital purposes and from community fundraising activities.

The My School website is a useful source for having a brief account of the main sources of income and actual dollar figures available to each individual school.

This chapter has presented the various avenues of school revenue which represent the autonomy enjoyed by schools in Victoria in terms of generating money at the local level, including various fundraising activities and trading operations. The effectiveness of the school leadership and the school council in generating revenue can decide the financial strength and strategic capability of the school.

Chapter 14

Expenditure Structure in Victorian Government Schools

Introduction

This chapter details the expenditure framework for Victorian government schools operating under an autonomous management system. It elucidates how funds are utilised, encompassing allocations for teaching and learning endeavours, maintenance of facilities, provision of student support services, and routine operational expenses. Expenditure considerations span both recurrent and capital projects.

Types of Expenditure in Government Schools

There are two types, or functions, of school expenditure known as recurrent and capital. Recurrent expenditure refers to the costs incurred to ensure the efficient and smooth operation of the school. In contrast, capital expenditure is money spent to buy or improve long-term fixed assets used for educational purposes, such as renovating classrooms or constructing a new library.

Recurrent Expenditure in Victorian Government Schools

Salaries and Allowances

These include salaries to locally employed staff, both teaching and non-teaching. The SRP provides credit to schools to cover teaching staff and the principal salaries from EduPay (the central payroll system), which is centrally managed at the Department level and not included in the individual school expenditure. Teaching staff include teachers for specialist programs like music, languages other than English, and other instructional roles. Non-teaching staff include support staff, administrative personnel, teacher aides, and other non-teaching roles.

Superannuation, WorkCover, Annual Leave, and Long Service Leave

- Superannuation: Employer contributions to a complying superannuation fund for staff employed by the School Council.
- WorkCover: Workers' compensation premiums for staff employed by School Councils (Local Payroll).
- Annual Leave: Provisions for eligible staff on the school-level payroll.

Bank Charges

This includes bank fees and charges related to school accounts, such as stop payment and dishonoured cheque fees.

Consumables

Costs for school-related consumables come under several categories:

- Office/Teacher Requisites: Stationery and other items for administrative or teaching services.
- Printing and Photocopying: Costs for printing and photocopying items used for teaching, administrative, or student purposes.
- Class Materials: Consumable materials for student use.
- Computer Software: All computer packages less than $5,000, including software applications and associated licenses.

Books and Publications

These include reference materials for teaching and non-teaching use, such as library books, periodicals, journals, subscriptions, and class sets of textbooks.

Communication Costs

This includes expenses for internet and associated costs, telephone and line rentals, internet replacement of cabling, repairs to telephone lines, and postage.

Advertising and Marketing

This includes the advertising and marketing activities to promote the school including electronic billboards, name boards, and marketing images.

Equipment/Maintenance/Hire

This category covers costs associated with office or classroom furniture, fittings, repairs, and maintenance of equipment, leased/hired equipment, motor vehicles, and various audio-visual items.

Utilities and Property Services

Utility costs include electricity, gas, water, sewerage charges, and local council rates. Property services costs include security, sanitation, contract cleaning, refuse and garbage disposal, building maintenance, and ground maintenance.

Travel and Subsistence" Costs associated with student and staff travel for school business, reimbursements for private vehicles, and meal allowances.

Motor Vehicle Expenses: Costs for purchasing, leasing, or renting motor vehicles and expenses related to operating school-owned motor vehicles and buses.

School Administration: Administration costs include advertising, insurance payments, subscriptions to professional bodies, and courier deliveries.

Health-Related Expenses: This category includes expenses for health services provided to students and staff, such as flu injections and first aid materials.

Professional Development: Costs associated with the professional development of school staff, including registration fees, venue hire, and organisation of conferences/workshops/seminars.

Entertainment and Hospitality: Schools are entitled to entertainment and hospitality expenses, which can include events like Christmas parties, retirement functions, meetings with refreshments, and more.

Trading and Fundraising: Costs associated with school council-managed trading operations and fundraising activities, excluding salaries and wages.

Other Expenses: This includes payments to technical support specialists, contractors and consultants, guest speakers, and costs associated with camps, excursions, and school-based activities.

Capital Expenditure

Capital expenditure involves the creation of fixed assets and the acquisition of land, buildings, and intangible assets. It includes expenses for long-term improvements to the school's operational capacity.

Capital Expenditure Items in Government Schools

In Victorian schools, capital expenditure relates to asset purchases with a value greater than $5,000. Examples include:
- New school buildings
- Computers/IT equipment, printers, and scanners
- Office equipment, furniture, and fittings
- Musical equipment
- Communication equipment
- Plant and equipment
- Sporting equipment
- Other assets

Capital and Maintenance Works

Each school is required to manage capital and maintenance work through an Asset Management Plan (AMP) with a five-year forward plan. Schools must complete this plan in conjunction with the Regional Office and the Infrastructure Division of the Department. Once a school's AMP is approved, priority projects identified in the AMP can begin implementation. Capital and maintenance works can be school-led or Department-led.

Project Categories

The Department has established four project budget categories for capital works and major maintenance, each with distinct compliance requirements:

- Category One – Under $25,000: Schools handle these projects independently after completing the Asset Management Plan (AMP), requiring one quote.
- Category Two – $25,000 to $200,000: Departmental approval is needed for projects over $50,000. Three quotes are required, and project management can be done by the school or a Principal Design Consultant.
- Category Three – $200,000 to $5 million: Requires a Principal Design Consultant for management, design, and cost planning. At least three tenders are needed to select a builder.
- Category Four – Over $5 million: Similar to Category Three, with an additional requirement for an independent quantity surveyor.

MySchool Website

The MySchool website lists capital expenditure for each school. The categories include:

- Australian Government Capital Expenditure: Funded by the Australian Government.
- State and Territory Government Capital Expenditure: Funded by state and territory governments.
- New School Loans: Capital expenditure funded by capital loan drawdowns (applicable to non-government schools).
- Income Allocated to Current Capital Projects: Gross income received by the school spent on capital projects.
- Other: Capital expenditure funded through other private sources, including retained earnings from previous years.

This chapter has presented the expenditure items of a school under normal operating circumstances under school autonomy.

Chapter 15

Resourcing Teaching Force: Workforce Management in Victorian Government Schools

Introduction

Chapter fifteen delineates the strategies for planning and sustaining an efficient teaching workforce within government schools operating under the principles of school autonomy. In a decentralised management framework, adept workforce planning becomes imperative for each educational institution's local objectives. Principals oversee staff deployment utilising funds earmarked for the school, primarily sourced from the Student Resource Package (SRP). This funding, constituting ninety percent of the SRP, is designated for schools' staffing requirements. Workforce management in Victorian schools essentially entails crafting staff composition within fiscal limits to realise strategic objectives.

Planning Process

The SRP budget for a school is determined by a formula based on student and school-related factors. It includes operating budgets encompassing credit and cash components. Approximately ninety percent of a school's SRP is credited for staff salaries, managed centrally. Schools can convert cash to credit with departmental approval to meet staffing needs. School strategic plans drive curriculum, budget, accountability, and workforce plans. Principals, within legislative boundaries, have delegated authority to manage staffing. A three- to five-year workforce plan is expected to align with the projected SRP. Efforts should be made to avoid exceeding the SRP allocation.

Systematic Approach

Workforce planning is a systematic process integrating workforce requirements, business objectives, budgets, and future needs. Principals are primarily responsible for workforce management, keeping the school council informed of staffing changes affecting the SRP.

Workforce planning must comply with legislative, policy, and procedural requirements, including departmental policies, teaching service orders, and industrial agreements. Local contextual factors such as enrollment projections, curriculum objectives, class size, and community expectations should be considered. Schools should devise short- and long-term workforce strategies which align with curriculum delivery, support teacher development, and address planned attrition. The Department's SRP Planner assists principals in guiding workforce planning by modelling enrollment and staffing scenarios.

This process is geared towards achieving the schools' strategic goals and priorities while effectively responding to anticipated future needs. To aid in this endeavour, the Department has devised a comprehensive Schools Workforce

Planning Guide. This resource assists schools in developing, implementing, and sustaining a tailored workforce profile and school structure that best suits their individual community needs. While applicable to all schools across Victoria, including those of varying sizes, locations, and specialisations, the Department also provides additional specialised advice for smaller and specialised schools.

In a dynamic educational landscape, workforce planning enables schools to remain responsive to emerging trends. Continuous review and adaptation ensure long-term sustainability.

Workforce Planning Process

The workforce planning process in schools involves several key phases to ensure alignment with the school's strategic goals and effective utilisation of resources. Here is a brief overview of the planning process:

- Phase 1: Analysing the Context: Understand school goals and student profiles. Use historical data to identify focus areas for workforce planning.
- Phase 2: Designing Future School: Create a vision for the school and workforce. Adjust staffing based on projections and education trends.
- Phase 3: Assessing Current Status: Evaluate current workforce against future needs. Identify gaps in skills or staffing.
- Phase 4: Implementing Workforce Strategy: Address gaps through recruitment, training, and development. Adjust strategies as needed.
- Phase 5: Monitoring and Review: Continuously assess the impact of workforce planning on operations and outcomes. Adjust plans to stay aligned with goals.

By following these phases of the workforce planning process, schools can proactively address staffing needs, optimise resource allocation, and create a workforce that is well-equipped to support the school's mission and provide high-quality education to students.

Consequences of a Lack of Effective Workforce Management

A shortage of qualified teachers in schools can negatively impact students, staff, and the learning environment. Lower academic performance may result from inadequate teaching quality, hindering students' full potential. Staff may experience increased workloads and burnout, leading to high turnover rates and instability. Insufficient staffing affects professional development opportunities, hindering teacher growth and skill development. Meeting diverse student needs becomes challenging, impacting academic support and accommodations. Implementation of school initiatives may suffer without qualified teachers, affecting strategic plans and desired outcomes. Prioritising workforce planning and recruitment is crucial to ensuring a qualified and effective teaching force, supporting student success.

Challenges in Workforce Management

The principal faces several management challenges when devising the workforce plan. Firstly, they must decide on the leadership profile, including the principal's grade, salary range, and the allocation of assistant principals. These positions are crucial but can consume a significant portion of the school's staff credits. Secondly, determining the teaching profile involves decisions on leading teachers, program coordinators, expert teachers, and graduate teachers to maintain a balanced arrangement. Enrollment numbers and trends impact staffing, with declining enrollments potentially leading to funding and position losses. Balancing support staff and teaching staff is crucial, as both play vital roles in school management. Retaining high-performing teachers, considering salary progression and introducing special curriculum programs, requires a stable and qualified teaching force. Succession plans become essential in cases where the teaching force has an older demographic.

Staff Costs and Legislative Obligations

Managing staff costs is crucial, covering expenses like superannuation, WorkCover payments, and leave provisions. Schools must allocate funds for these compulsory benefits, as mandated by laws such as the Superannuation Guarantee Act 1992. Workforce planning should also address annual and long service leave requirements for eligible staff, constituting provisional expenses. Compliance with legislative obligations regarding occupational health and safety, workplace injury rehabilitation, and worker rights is essential. Employers, including school councils, must adhere to laws like the Accident Compensation Act 1985 and contribute to WorkSafe premiums for a safe workplace.

By following a systematic approach to workforce planning, schools can ensure they have a well-equipped and efficient teaching force to meet their strategic objectives and provide high-quality education.

Part V

Executive Blueprint: Governance Framework in Victoria

Chapter 16

Unveiling the School Governance Model in Victoria

Introduction

This chapter provides an overview of the devolved school governance system in Victoria, elucidating the governance structures and decision-making responsibilities entrusted to school councils. It examines the dynamic between school councils and principals, underscoring the councils' position as statutory entities answerable to the Minister. The chapter illuminates the collaborative endeavours anticipated between the community and school administration, facilitated by school councils, to realise the student outcomes delineated in the school's strategic blueprint.

Victorian School Governance Model

All schools, whether government or non-government, fall within the jurisdiction of the Victorian Department of Education and Training, which offers guidance to the Minister for Education. They are registered with the Victorian Registration and Qualification Authority (VRQA) and are obliged to meet minimum standards stipulated by the Education and Training Reform Act 2006.

The state is divided into four regional education offices (North Eastern Region, North Western Region, South Eastern Region, and South Western Region), acting as intermediaries between the Department and schools. These offices collaborate with schools, communities, and other stakeholders to ensure optimal educational outcomes. Regional Directors play a pivotal role in supporting schools and evaluating their performance.

Under the governance of school councils, which are distinct legal entities, schools are held accountable to the Minister for Education. Designated as public entities under the Public Administration Act 2004, these councils adhere to regulations, requirements, and standards delineated within the Act. This accountability extends to transparent operations and responsible use of public funds and resources.

Governed by the Act, school councils adhere to specified governance standards, including decision-making processes, conflict of interest management, and financial oversight. Mechanisms for oversight and scrutiny, such as audits or investigations, ensure adherence to relevant legislation.

The Principal

The principal is the accountable officer of the school, responsible to the Secretary (through the regional director) for financial accounting and reporting, effectiveness of audits, and effective use of resources. They are the executive officer of the school council and are responsible for implementing school council decisions.

The principal has the overall responsibility for the education provided to the students, while leading the development with a broad direction, vision, and strategic plan of the school where the school council is actively involved in this process. The principal has an educational leadership role and a clear set of accountabilities in relation to the operation of the school. The principal is responsible for providing the school council with timely advice about educational and other matters, reporting annually to the school council on the school's performance against its strategic plan, and ensuring that action is taken on the council's decisions.

Figure 8: Victorian School Governance Model

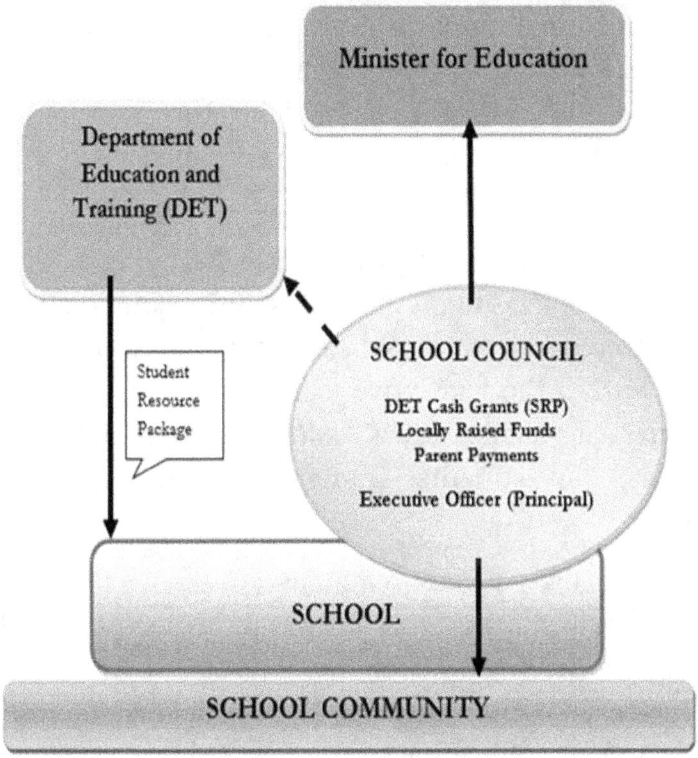

School Councils and Functions

Each school council is established as a legal entity under an order made by the Minister of Education pursuant to section 2.3.2 of the Education and Training Reform Act 2006. This order outlines the council's composition, objectives, powers, functions, and accountabilities, as well as the role of its executive officer. Members of the school council are bound by the Director's Code of Conduct established under the Public Administration Act 2004 and are indemnified against any liability incurred while carrying out their duties.

The primary role of the school council is to support the effective governance of the school, ensuring that decisions made prioritise the best interests of the students and enhance their educational opportunities. As legal entities, school councils have broad powers, including entering contracts, employing staff, charging fees, delegating powers, selling property, and providing preschool programs.

The school strategic plan serves as a roadmap for the school's direction over the next four years, guiding improvements in student outcomes and resource allocation. School councils are responsible for developing various policies within the legislative framework and departmental guidelines, covering areas such as parent payments, complaints, investments, student engagement, and safety protocols.

Additionally, school councils oversee the school's financial performance, ensuring proper expenditure of funds and implementing effective internal controls. They collaborate with the principal to develop and monitor the school budget, allocating resources to key improvement strategies outlined in the strategic plan. Many school councils establish finance sub-committees to manage routine financial tasks effectively.

Membership of School Councils

There are three member categories:

- Parent Member: Parents or guardians of enrolled students can nominate themselves.
- School Employee Member: Teachers, staff, and administrators can nominate themselves.
- Student Member: Some councils include student representation. Student members, usually enrolled students, provide a student viewpoint.

These categories ensure diverse representation and perspectives, enhancing governance and decision-making in the school community.

School Strategic Plan

The School Strategic Plan outlines the school's vision and objectives for the next four years, aiming to enhance student outcomes. Mandated by the Education Training and Reform Act 2006 Section 2.3.24, subsection (1), it details the school's goals, targets, and strategies for achievement.

The process, guided by the School Accountability and Improvement Framework (DET, 2012), involves:

- Evaluating the current strategic plan's performance
- Formulating a new four-year plan, encompassing the school's purpose, values, environmental context, goals, targets, and improvement strategies
- Creating annual implementation plans to detail the execution and monitoring of key strategies

Publishing an annual report to communicate successes and challenges to the school community Each school develops an annual implementation plan aligned with the four-year strategic plan, with both plans requiring endorsement by the school council.

Annual Report to the Community

Each school produces an annual report for the school community, mandated by the Education and Training Reform Act 2006. This report serves to inform the community about the school's achievements and performance, offering insights for future planning. It follows a standardised template outlined by the Department of Education and Training (DET, 2013f) and typically includes:

- School Statement: Discusses the school's performance and future directions briefly.
- Summary of Performance: Presents key performance indicators for student outcomes in achievement, engagement, and wellbeing, along with comparative data from other government schools.
- Financial Performance Summary: Provides an overview of the school's financial performance and position for the year, ensuring transparency and accountability in the use of school funds.

The annual report is accessible to all members of the school community. Additionally, school councils are legally obligated to host a public meeting each year, during which the annual report is presented for community review and discussion.

The school council is a legal entity responsible for the strategic directions of the school and overseeing the school financial management.

Chapter 17

Managing Financial & Operational Risks in Victorian Government Schools

Introduction

With a devolved financial management and governance system, Victorian government schools bear the responsibility of overseeing finances at the local level, overseen by school councils. This chapter delineates various systems and strategies advocated for implementation in government schools to address financial risks. It elaborates on methods including policy development, regular monitoring, internal controls, financial audits, and transparent reporting to the school community.

Policy Development

Policy development represents a crucial responsibility of school councils in Victoria, Australia. It is a powerful instrument that enables school councils to extend their influence and powers. These councils are tasked with creating and refining policies that guide operations and decision-making processes within the school, ensuring consistency, fairness, and legal compliance.

Policy development involves crafting guidelines and procedures governing various aspects of school operations, such as student conduct, curriculum design, staff recruitment, and financial management. Collaboratively, school councils work with key stakeholders to align policies with the school's values, vision, and objectives.

The benefits of policy development are numerous. It fosters consistency, fairness, and equity across the school community while promoting clarity through clearly articulated expectations and guidelines. Policies also ensure compliance with legal requirements, enhance accountability by defining roles and responsibilities, and streamline processes to improve efficiency.

The policy development process begins with identifying areas requiring policy formulation or revision based on school priorities, legal mandates, and stakeholder feedback. School councils gather information, research best practices, and engage relevant stakeholders to craft draft policies that align with the school's values and community needs. Stakeholder feedback is sought to ensure inclusivity and relevance. Finalised policies are then approved by the school council, communicated to stakeholders, and implemented within the school community.

In Victoria, the policy development and review function of school councils are integral to governance and decision-making processes. By establishing clear policies reflective of the school's ethos, councils provide a consistent framework for decision-making, enhance accountability, and ensure compliance with legal standards. Regular policy review allows for adaptation to evolving circumstances, addressing emerging issues, and fostering continuous improvement within the school environment.

Financial Management

School funds, being public funds, are governed by the Financial Management Act 1994 (Vic), ensuring public accountability in budget planning, allocation, and utilisation. Schools also adhere to various financial acts such as the A New Tax System (Goods and Services Tax) Act 1999, Fringe Benefits Tax Act 1986, and Income Tax Assessment Act 1997.

The school council spearheads the budget development process by reviewing submissions, identifying programs supporting the strategic plan, and approving the school budget. Additionally, the council assesses additional funding from fundraising activities, approves related programs and events, and contributes to the parent payments policy within departmental guidelines.

Regular financial reports are requested and monitored against the budget, with action taken to address arising issues. The council ensures sound internal controls, appointing a councillor, usually the President, to approve payments and sign checks.

In summary, financial management in schools is a joint responsibility of the School Principal and the School Council, ensuring compliance with legislative requirements, strategic alignment, and effective internal controls.

Regular Monitoring and Review

Regular monitoring is essential for school councils to ensure that all projected revenue and expenditures are accounted for and align with the budget. This involves comparing actual figures with budgeted ones to assess performance against expectations. Variances are identified, investigated, and reported, enabling remedial action at the school council level.

Two key reports aid in financial performance monitoring: the operating statement and the balance sheet. The operating statement depicts operating results over a specific period, providing a monthly and year-to-date comparison of revenue and expenditure, akin to an income or profit and loss statement. Monitoring this report allows identification of surplus or deficit on a monthly or year-to-date basis, facilitating action such as budget revisions or expenditure restrictions in underperforming areas.

While school principals manage approximately 90 percent of the total school budget, school councils oversee the management of the cash budget, around 10 percent of the allocation. Additionally, the staffing composition is subject to school council approval.

The balance sheet offers insights into the school's financial position, detailing assets and liabilities, with both sides balancing out. It provides a snapshot of the financial health and major accounts, clarifying the purpose and composition of each account. Negative figures indicate credit balances, while positive ones represent debit balances.

Information from the operating statement and balance sheet informs budget adjustments to accurately reflect the school's financial position. The finance sub-committee and council review whether revenue and expenditure targets are met, with significant variations prompting action, subject to school council approval.

Various reports, including balance sheet specific period, operating statement, cash flow statement, bank account movements, cash receipts, cash payments, and overall Student Resource Package (SRP) position, are presented monthly to the finance committee or school council. These reports, certified by the principal and school council president, offer insights into the school's financial health and SRP status.

Internal Controls

Internal controls are systematic measures established by an organisation to conduct its business in an orderly and efficient manner. They comprise a broad framework of processes, procedures, systems, and strategies that an organisation has put in place to ensure the successful delivery of its programs. All organisations meet with a degree of risk in chasing their goals and priorities. The management must ensure the effectiveness of the company's internal controls over financial reporting on an appropriate, acceptable control framework, established by a body of experts.

A major responsibility of the school council under the Education and Training Reform Act 2006 is to "ensure that all monies coming into the hands of the council are used for proper purposes." The internal control systems play a major part in fulfilling this function.

Internal controls are the procedures that the schools implement, to ensure that monies coming into the school are being spent as planned, that the school assets are safe, and the council can rely on the accuracy of the financial information.

An integral part of control assessment is the analysis of risk. All organisations encounter a degree of risk in the pursuit of their goals and priorities. The internal control systems and mechanisms reduce the risk and highlight the planning or operational weakness. An important part of the internal control framework of a school is financial management and its related operational elements, for example, the internal controls applying to receipts, payments, custody, and control of assets, salaries, wages, and other benefits, bank accounts, and investments.

Internal controls vary between schools. Schools that do not have appropriate controls face higher risks than those that do. For example, in an organisation where the same person receives cash, issues receipts, prepares the banking, does the actual banking, and carries out bank reconciliations, the risk of a possible cash misappropriation is usually higher than in an organisation where these duties are split between two or more people. The appropriate operation of school accounts, sound budgeting and monitoring processes, and appropriate classification of receipts and payments greatly strengthen the financial internal control environment in schools.

The external audit of a school complements the internal control environment by providing the school with a report on the operation of the controls and highlighting areas, via management letters to the school council and the principal, where changes and/or improvements may be required. The School Council Financial Audit program is described in the section after the next.

Types of Internal Controls Available for School Councils

There are many types of internal controls (preventive, detective, and corrective) that provide an assurance of security and proper functioning of the accounting system.

The major controls can be broadly classified under the following headings:

- Policy: This type of control includes a clear plan of the organisation, together with written position descriptions that define and allocate the roles and responsibilities of the staff. It prevents both inefficient and overlapping functions and the avoidance of responsibility in some areas. Any delegation of authority and responsibility should be clearly shown.
- Segregation of Duties: This internal control is designed to separate those responsibilities or duties, which, if combined, would enable an individual person to process and record a complete transaction, such as ordering, receiving, approving, and paying for goods. Functions that should be separated include authorisation, payment, custody, and recording.
- Physical Controls: These are measures that are taken to safeguard assets, including property, stores, cash, and buildings. Many schools in Victoria have installed security alarm systems and CCTV cameras for surveillance.
- Delegation, Authorisation, and Approval: The delegation of authority to authorise expenditure is provided by the school council. All transactions should be authorised or approved by a responsible person, who is familiar with the program budget requirements.
- Accounting Controls: These are the controls within the record-keeping function, which are designed to provide reasonable assurance that all transactions have been properly authorised, the data is accurately recorded, and the accounting records are reconciled.

- Personnel: This internal control covers staff training and competencies. Principals should ensure that the administrative staff has sufficient knowledge and expertise to follow the approved policies and position descriptions.
- Supervision and Oversight: A good system of internal control must include provision for supervision and oversight. This can be facilitated by an internal checking system, where the work of one person and steps in the process are automatically checked by another. This can be further strengthened by a system of 'spot checking' random areas. The school council, through the school, has the ultimate responsibility to ensure that controls are in place and compliance is being achieved.
- Electronic Security: Electronic security must be designed to prevent unauthorised access to systems, software, and data. Secure passwords, security tokens, and access roles limit access to transactions and data to those required by individuals and authorised for their use.
- Physical Security: Physical security must be designed to prevent unauthorised access to school assets and accounting records. Examples of physical security include a safe, vault, locked doors/desk drawers, and card key systems.
- Employee Background Checks: This includes the Department's recruitment checks as well as requiring all teaching staff (including CRTs) to have a current Victorian Institute of Teaching (VIT) registration, all non-teaching staff to have a current Working with

Children Check and all employees who handle cash to have undertaken a criminal record check.
- Employee Training and Professional Development: Having a well-trained, competent workforce that allows role rotation of staff will provide opportunities for multi-skilling and will enhance the internal control system of the school. For example, specific 'how to' training will support hard controls such as processing accuracy and information quality while values and induction type training will support soft controls as they will set out desirable behaviours and reinforce morale.

School Council Financial Audit

Despite the school councils being public (legal) entities, the Education and Training Reform Act 2006 does not require that the annual financial statements of school councils be independently audited. Nor are school councils required to table their individual annual reports (i.e., audited financial statements) in Parliament.

However, the legislation provides the opportunity for the Secretary of the Department (head of the Department) to ensure that an effective 'quality assurance' system is in place to control the financial and operational activities of the school councils. Under this requirement, the Department of Education and Training conducts financial audits at least once every three years in every school. The selection of schools for this audit is based on risk criteria. This means that approximately two-thirds of the schools are not audited every year and, therefore, independent guarantee of soundness and control of school finances are not available. Even though legislation allows for school financial statements to be consolidated into the Department's annual report to Parliament, there are gaps in an audit and assurance of a school's financial statements.

All Victorian Government school councils undergo an independent financial audit of school council accounts at least once every three years. High-risk schools are subject to audit every year. Schools should have their financial statements completed and available for audit by 31 December each year. Audits are carried out during the period from January to March and have to be completed by 30 April.

The objectives of the audit are to provide reasonable assurance over the financial activities under the direct control of the school councils. The auditors are required to form a view on the school's annual financial statements. They have to present a qualified report when they discover irregular accounting practices. Auditors also prepare a management letter for the information of the principal and school council, with any specific matters that require further attention by the school council. Principals are required to provide a management response to auditors and implement these audit recommendations.

The Department conducts a number of regular, targeted, and ad hoc audits, reviews, and other assurance activities in Victorian government schools. The purpose of these assurance activities depends on the specific activity (for example, OHS, financial assurance, enrolment data verification) but is typically required to meet legislative, compliance, and risk management requirements.

On occasion, the Department may conduct targeted, ad hoc, or other audits and reviews for specific reasons or at the request of the school. External agencies such as the Victorian

Auditor General's Office may also conduct audits in relation to government schools. These are out of scope for this summary. The Department conducts a number of audits, reviews, and other assurance activities in Victorian government schools. The purpose of these assurance activities depends on the specific activity (for example, OHS, financial assurance, enrolment data verification) but is typically required to meet legislative, compliance, and risk management requirements.

This chapter has presented the key functions of the school council, which are budgeting and financial planning. Several steps in the budget planning process have been explained to ensure that the school is involved in a practical and effective school budget development process. To manage the school finance effectively, the school leadership and school councils have to be aware of the various internal controls that are available to them. The School Council Financial Audit Program is available to the school, school council, the Department, and the Minister for Education, to ensure reasonable assurance of public investment in the school.

Part VI

Gloomy Horizon of Outcomes: Emerging Challenges & Unanticipated Consequences

Chapter 18

School Autonomy: Challenges in Financial Management & Governance in Victoria

Introduction

Chapter eighteen examines the challenges encountered by government schools operating under school autonomy. It discusses potential pitfalls in financial management, such as budget deficits, mismatches between strategic plans and staff profiles, losses from trading operations, inefficient use of finance software like CASES21, and unaccountable financial systems that may lead to misappropriation.

Potential Lapses of Devolved Financial Management

The following section explains a number of potential lapses that can emerge as a result of the operations of the devolved financial management system and consequently can go against the intentions of the system.

Budget Deficit

School level budgeting and financial management is a key component of the devolved financial management in

Victoria. For a favourable budget the available funds must be equal or greater than the expected expenditure. Budget deficit means that the expenses are greater than the revenue. This situation can arise when there is overspending, contrary to the planned expenditure or under-delivery of the expected revenue. Among the factors for the budget deficit may include the collection of less than expected local fundraising money and misappropriation of funds. A budget deficit can put pressure on the delivery of the strategic plan and disruption of the education delivery. In a situation like this the Department provides cash advances or finance rescue packages to those schools until the budget comes under control.

Even though the schools can be rescued by providing cash advances by the Department, a budget deficit breaks down the fundamental purpose of local budgeting. This situation restricts the school's capacity to address local educational performance issues effectively.

Bad budgeting and financial management in the Victorian government schools does not mean they will become bankrupt or financially broke. In accounting terms, if revenue meets or exceeds the expenses regularly, the school is financially solvent. This is a favourable scenario, that is, they have a budget surplus. However, when expenses start to exceed the revenues, the school will potentially be heading toward financial difficulty. This is an unfavourable scenario, where it is generally stated that the school has a budget deficit. Budget deficit is potentially a result of ineffective budgeting and financial planning. In such situations, the Victorian Department of Education and Training (DET), intervene, and may provide cash advances to bring the budget into balance. The Department also provides assistance to achieve long-term recovery and sustainability.

Mismatch Between the Strategic Plan and Staff Profile

As presented in previous chapters eighty percent of SRP money is allocated to schools for staff salaries. Principals and school councils are required to develop an appropriate staff mix to fit with the schools strategic and educational directions. A mismatch between the strategic plan and staff profile puts pressure on delivery of the education program. In Victoria, the devolved school management system anticipates local strategy for the advancement of student outcomes. A mismatch can create deficiencies in the strategic plan and/or school staff mix.

It is also to be understood that when there is no effective planning with reasonable strategies, the strategic plan could be unrealistic and ineffective. Then, whether the staff profile is accurate or not, the achievement of student outcomes cannot be realised. At the same time, if the staff profile is not adequate to deliver the strategic plan and its priorities, for example, if the staff mix is top heavy or bottom heavy, with no adequate experienced or qualified teachers, then it makes difficult to deliver the plan.

Losses from Trading Operations and Fundraising Activities

Victorian devolved school governance model provided opportunities to raise local funds including running trading operations at schools. School level trading operations can include school canteen, uniform shop and outside school hours childcare programs. Trading operations should make a profit or very least achieve break even. If the trading operations are running at a loss or in a trend of losing profits, then that breaks down the very purpose of the operation. There will be several reasons for losses, including, misappropriations, inadequate monitoring, and more spending, such as, extensive Labour/payroll etc. Furthermore, intense competition for services by other providers or a lack of demand can also contribute to a loss.

Losing a trading operation will result in subsidising from other programs. This is not an ideal situation for school councils. Using profit and loss statements, the school councils should assess the possible reasons for the loss and the validity of continuing the operation. A decision to subsidise a trading operation has to be approved and documented by the school council.

Fundraising activities are always anticipated to generate funds. Many fundraising activities involve costs. If the gain is less or lower than expected, the purpose of the fundraising effort can be futile. Fundraising activities are always to be used to generate maximum benefit with fewer expenses. Some school programs may depend on local funding. Inadequate fundraising could disrupt the planned educational deliverable that depends on additional local funding.

Ineffective Use of School Financial Management Software – CASES21 Finance

CASES21 Finance is the integrated school administration and finance software system used in government schools in Victoria. It was introduced in 2000, followed by a full rollout in 2006. It is designed to provide government schools in Victoria with a standardised system wherewith to manage their core administrative and financial matters. The software is also intended to help schools provide data reports to the Department. This system provides school staff with secure access to data entry and reporting modules that support the broad range of school administration and their financial functions.

CASES21 Finance is a hybrid system that sits between cash and accrual accounting systems. Therefore, some issues relating to its application for financial management and reporting decisions have been raised. The major issue with this system lies in its complexity and its technical nature and, therefore, many school principals do not have a good grasp of the system. It is expected that the school's business managers need to be skilled in the use and operation of the system, but the level of expertise among these business managers is inconsistent. Given the complexity of the system, it presents some difficulties for the school authorities to monitor their finances on a regular basis. Further, the inherent complexity provides opportunities for dishonest people to manipulate it for fraudulent purposes. A lack of consistent business acumen of the school principals increases such opportunities.

Unaccountable Financial Systems at Schools

School councils in Victoria are only accountable for overseeing the finances of the school. Within the system of devolved financial management in Victoria, funds can be inappropriately transferred by state and regional program areas and disbursed by schools with inadequate supervision by the school council. This presented a grave risk of fraud and corruption.

In April 2013, the Victorian Independent Broad-Based Anti-Corruption Commission (IBAC) held an inquiry (an open public investigation) into funds inappropriately allocated to a number of schools for discretionary use outside the established norms and mechanisms of accountability. This group of schools is known as "Banker Schools" or "Program Coordinator Schools". Under this process, unexpended funds were retained in the schools' bank accounts, and remained there uncommitted. The evidence presented to the inquiry indicated that there have been widespread instances of systemic corruption in the use and application of these funds. Details of this IBAC examination code that was named Operation Ord are available at the IBAC webpage. It is worthwhile examining the background of this funding component and its potential implications.

The IBAC inquiry, in particular, focused on:

- The alleged involvement of DET staff in the establishment of banker schools or program coordinator schools, the allocation of funds to schools for goods and services that were not always provided, and the misuse of the department's funds.
- Whether DET staff (or their associates), and school principals and business managers received financial or other benefits as a result.
- The family and business connections between DET staff (or their associates), school principals and business managers, and the suppliers of goods and services.
- DET systems and practices around procurement, financial management and allocation of funding, and the awarding of contracts (IBAC, 2015).

For nearly two decades, program coordinator schools in Victoria managed funds for collaborative educational programs and staff development across school clusters.

However, until January 2015, there were no formal governance arrangements for these funds. The Department of Education and Training (DET) then clarified the program's purpose to manage specific programs funded by schools, regional offices, and central offices. Before these arrangements, financial audits and reporting often overlooked these funds, enabling discretionary use and hiding unspent funds from state budget processes.

The Independent Broad-based Anti-corruption Commission (IBAC) inquiry revealed that senior Department executives arranged for school principals at program coordinator schools to transfer large sums to their school accounts, subsequently paying invoices without verifying the delivery of goods or services. This violated normal financial management policies and the Education and Training Reform Act 2006, which mandates that school councils make payments solely for the school's benefit. The inquiry found that these practices led to the misuse of funds, including improper gifts, extravagant parties, and unnecessary overseas travel for officials and their associates.

Recognising these systemic flaws, the Department ceased most centrally and regionally funded program coordinator school arrangements, except where existing binding contracts required continuation. They also began recovering uncommitted and unspent funds from these schools' accounts. This response aimed to address the lack of necessary controls and ensure better accountability for public funds, preventing further misuse. The IBAC inquiry highlighted the need for strict governance and transparency to safeguard educational resources and maintain public trust.

Chapter 19

School Autonomy: Unanticipated Financial Irregularities & Unethical Practices in Victoria

Introduction

Although most schools effectively manage their local finances, there have been reports of financial irregularities and unethical conduct in some schools operating under the devolved governance and financial management framework. This chapter traces these issues, providing an overview of reported conduct and potential internal control lapses that have contributed to them. It also describes the integrity reform initiatives developed by the Department to mitigate these issues.

Community Expectations

The community expects high standards of integrity, impartiality, and responsible use of public resources by public officials. Further, public officials are expected to earn and sustain public trust; be honest, open, and transparent in their dealings; make decisions and provide advice without bias; avoid any real or perceived conflict of interest; and use their powers responsibly. The devolution of financial management responsibilities to the local level opens potential opportunities for dishonest people to commit white-collar crimes.

Delegation of financial responsibility and decisions to schools can prima facie increase the possibility of financial irregularity, as many more officials have direct access to funds and are involved in decision-making. Whether or not devolved school management itself influences financial irregularities is relatively unknown. However, in Victoria, reported school-related financial irregularities include cash misappropriation, fraudulent use of school credit cards, internet banking fraud, kickbacks from suppliers, theft of assets, inflated enrollment, falsification of invoices, and conflicts of interest in recruiting and contracting.

Financial Irregularities, Unethical practices and Risks

The following section lists publicly reported financial irregularities and unethical practices reported in news papers and integrity agency reports (for example, Herald Sun, 2014; Sunday Herald Sun, 2012; The Age, 2012, 2023; The Sunday Age, 2012; The Australian, 2011a, 2011b; Victorian Ombudsman, 2011; 2020; Victorian Institute of Teaching, 2010; Levacic and Downes, 2004; IBAC, 2015; The Educator, 2023).

Misappropriation of Cash

Victorian government schools receive cash from parent payments, extracurricular activities, fundraising, donations, trading operations like school canteens, uniform shops, before- and after-hour school care programs, and book sales. Cash transactions are recognised as the most vulnerable area for schools. The risk of misappropriation of cash in schools has been confirmed by international research.

To ensure efficient and effective cash handling and manage the risk of fraud, the Victorian Department has developed best practices for internal controls. These include processing cash through CASES21, issuing official receipts, segregating duties, having two people count cash, encouraging the use of cheques, credit cards, and electronic funds transfer at points of sale, frequent banking, monthly bank reconciliations, regular oversight by the principal, and reporting to and monitoring by the school council. The school council plays a major role in managing cash misappropriation risks.

Irregular Tendering for Maintenance and Capital Work

The school council has the power to enter contracts with suppliers, conduct school maintenance work using SRP funds, complete capital work using locally raised funds, and complete capital projects using special grants. School council's and principal's financial delegation is limited to $50,000. Projects over $50,000 require departmental involvement.

Risks in tendering involve circumventing the tender process to give unfair advantage to a particular provider, unfair trading, ineffective tender evaluation processes, and conflicts of interest in awarding contracts. There is also the risk of schools underestimating or overestimating service values, causing a loss to the Department. DET has well-established procedures and guidelines for procurement, including purchasing thresholds, with exceptions for mandated Whole of Government Contracts policy.

The Department expects adherence to recommended procedures, including a tender evaluation panel with an independent member, proper tender evaluation, effective conflict of interest management, and seeking assistance and advice from the Regional Education Office or the Infrastructure and Sustainability Division of the Department. School council oversight is also crucial.

Irregular Internet and Electronic Banking

School councils can maintain multiple bank accounts, but the Department recommends two main accounts: the official account for operating funds and the High Yield Investment Account (HYIA) for cash flow planning and surplus funds investment. All school accounts, except the HYIA, must be in the school council's name, with registered signatories including the principal and a second co-signatory from the school council.

Risks include fraudulent internet banking, such as transferring school funds to personal accounts of school staff under the guise of refunds for parents, and unauthorised fund transfers by falsifying principals' signatures or passwords. Internal control lapses, such as sharing banking login details and passwords, have been identified.

Recommended internal controls include safe keeping of login names and passwords, user access control, daily limits on cash transfers, no refunds for parents through electronic funds transfer, review of monthly bank statements, monthly bank reconciliations, and regular oversight and monitoring by the principal and school council.

Inflated Student Enrollments

A student-based funding allocation model is susceptible to fraudulent and inflated student enrollments. Schools may report more students than are enrolled or higher indicators of need than actually exist to secure more funding. This constitutes falsification of enrollment numbers and ghost students to claim additional SRP allocations. Fraudulent reporting of enrollment data causes a school to receive more than its entitlement.

Irregular Purchasing Practices

In Victoria, school councils are empowered to purchase or maintain goods, equipment, and materials for carrying out their functions. A Purchasing Card Facility has been approved by the Minister, allowing for better cash flow management, reduced documentation, enhanced purchasing processes, and improved internal controls. However, purchasing cards can be fraudulently used for private expenses.

Risks include purchasing goods and services for private use, fraudulent use of purchasing cards, delivering goods to employees' private addresses, and fraudulent personal expense claims, including unauthorised travel. Fictitious invoices, duplicate invoices, and splitting invoices contrary to DET guidelines are also fraud risks.

Internal controls to prevent these practices include compulsory advertising of vacancies, a recruitment panel, effective conflict of interest management, recording the recruitment process and decision, merit protection training for recruitment panel members, qualification vetting, checking for a criminal record, management of casual relief teacher rosters, approved and signed timesheets, and payroll verification by a person before approval by the principal.

Misuse of School Assets

Schools have substantial investments in stores, equipment, furniture, books, and other learning materials. Proper procedures must be followed for purchase, custody, loss, or disposal of these items. Assets valued over $5,000 must be recorded in the School Asset Register, and items under $5,000, such as computers and audiovisual equipment, should also be recorded.

Risks include inappropriate use of school assets for private purposes and theft of assets by school employees. Controls include annual stocktaking of assets, safe keeping of attractive assets, and preparing and monitoring a list of assets borrowed by school staff.

Conflicts of Interest

A conflict of interest arises when an employee's public duty is influenced, or appears to be influenced, by a private interest. It can be actual, potential, or perceived. Public sector employees must declare and avoid conflicts of interest to maintain community trust and confidence.

Conflicts of interest are an inevitable fact of organisational life and can arise without anyone being at fault.

The Department's COI management relies on four principles: protecting the public interest, ensuring transparency and accountability, promoting individual responsibility for integrity and impartiality, and fostering an organisational culture that encourages effective COI management. Internal controls include requiring public sector employees to declare conflicts of interest, ensuring personal or financial interests do not influence their role, and managing conflicts transparently.

Reported conflicts of interest in Victorian schools have primarily involved recruitment, purchasing practices, and contracting.

Integrity Reforms

The Victorian Department of Education and Training (DET) has established a comprehensive fraud and corruption control framework to report, investigate and mitigate fraud and corruption risks.

Following the IBAC investigations uncovering various irregularities, the Department has implemented further extensive integrity reform initiatives since 2017. These include establishing a robust Integrity Division and strengthening a dedicated Fraud and Corruption Control unit.

The Fraud, Corruption, and Other Losses Policy 2021 outlines multiple reporting obligations aligned with IBAC requirements.

- **Public Interest Disclosures**: Under the Public Interest Disclosures Act 2012, the Department is mandated to establish procedures for reporting and handling disclosures. A designated Public Interest Disclosure Coordinator is in charge.
- **Mandatory Notifications:** The Independent Broad-based Anti-Corruption Commission Act 2011 requires the Department's Secretary to notify IBAC of any suspected corrupt conduct, regardless of severity or systemic nature.

- **Reporting of Significant or Systemic Incidents:** In accordance with the Standing Directions, the Department must report all cases of significant or systemic fraud, corruption, and other losses to the Responsible Minister, the Department's Audit and Risk Committee, and the Victorian Auditor-General.
- **Criminal Offenses:** Instances of internal and external fraud, theft, or other criminal offenses resulting in financial loss to the Department or a school council must be promptly reported to Victoria Police.
- **Recording of Fraud, Corruption, and Losses:** All employees are required to notify the Integrity, Assurance, and Executive Services Division (IAESD) of any instances of fraud, corruption, or other losses. Reporting avenues include contacting the Fraud and Corruption Control Unit via phone or email, informing their principal or manager for further coordination with the Fraud and Corruption Control Unit, or utilising the Speak Up service, available 24/7 to provide an independent platform for reporting.

Principals, as executive officers of school councils, bear additional responsibilities under the Independent Broad-based Anti-Corruption Commission Act 2011 (Vic). They are mandated to report any suspected corrupt conduct related to school councils or school council employees to IBAC.

Consequences

The school autonomy-related financial systems gave rise to IBAC's first large-scale investigations in Victoria since its inception in 2013. Operation Ord, which began in 2013, investigated allegations that senior departmental officers corruptly misappropriated funds from the Department of Education's budget. This included funds allocated to state primary and secondary schools through mechanisms such as false and inflated invoicing and the arrangement of inappropriate expenses like excessive hospitality, travel, and personal items. In 2016, Operation Dunham followed, probing further into the misappropriation of funds by senior officials in the Department of Education and Training. These investigations culminated in criminal charges being laid.

The Operation Ord investigation was pivotal in establishing IBAC's legitimacy as a major public integrity body alongside the Victorian Ombudsman and Auditor General's Office. The investigations received substantial media coverage due to their high-profile nature and the involvement of corrupt public service officials. This media attention, combined with the sensitive nature of the subject matter, prompted significant integrity reforms. These reforms introduced new policy changes, several awareness campaigns and training programs particularly targeting school principals and School Business Managers. The principals have been emphasised with new reporting requirements, regulatory and compliance requirements.

These reforms involved allocating public funds to establish massive and comprehensive integrity units and creating extensive investigating, reporting and monitoring systems. Consequently, a significant number of officials with expertise were recruited into the Victorian public service to manage the legal complexities of these reforms. New integrity officials enforced a zero-tolerance policy toward fraud and corruption, introducing universal programs to mitigate risks and ensure compliance across all public servants. However, the reformers struggled to identify high-risk areas for a targeted approach without unnecessary emphasis and disruption. Consequently, these stringent compliance requirements posed challenges for school leaders, often seeming disconnected from the core educational mission of teaching and learning.

Chapter 20

School Autonomy in Victoria: Unanticipated Governance Challenges

Introduction

This chapter analyses the impact and governance challenges arising from school autonomy reforms in Victorian government schools. These challenges, which are largely unanticipated consequences, stem from the inherent nature of autonomous and devolved governance. They are identified in relation to the roles of principals, teachers, and school councils.

Autonomy or Isolation

School autonomy can contribute to the increasing isolation of schools due to anticipated competition among schools. Under this model, schools operate as self-contained, self-managed entities, with little encouragement for collaboration. This independence can lead to fragmentation, leaving schools to navigate the market mechanisms that determine their success or failure. The strength of a school largely depends on the composition and configuration of local elements, including school leadership, local socioeconomic status, parental cultural capital, parental aspirations, realistic educational targets, and the availability of quality teaching staff.

Quality school leadership is essential to assemble all these elements cohesively. However, questions arise about the right configuration of local elements that can uplift and invigorate each school in different contexts. Can educational leaders get the configuration right and sustain motivation and endurance in environments with variable control? What additional support can be tapped into? What are the alternatives to discourage market forces? The biggest hurdle for educational leaders in school autonomy is to avoid the slippery slope of isolation, abandonment, and stagnation.

Demand for Good Governance More Than Ever

School autonomy underscores the importance of good governance more than ever before. When decision-making authority is decentralised to local schools and governing bodies like school councils, the need for good governance becomes heightened. Accountability stands out as a cornerstone of good governance, with devolution placing greater responsibility on school principals, teachers, and school councillors to be accountable to their local communities. However, there is a perception that policymakers and intermediate layers do not equally share this accountability burden, leaving schools subjected to continuous public scrutiny.

Transparency is another essential aspect of governance. Parents and the local community should have visibility into the decision-making processes within schools. They should understand how decisions are made, what information and advice are considered, and which legislative requirements and policies are adhered to. Schools must keep the community fully informed about decisions, processes, and outcomes to foster transparency.

Furthermore, genuine participation and consultation are vital for good governance. The community should have ample opportunities to participate in decision-making processes. By adhering to these principles of good governance, schools can evolve into open, transparent, and democratic institutions. This fosters community confidence and contributes to enhanced solidarity and welfare, ultimately preventing potential disengagement from educational matters within communities.

Demand for Marketing Schools and Promoting

Under the framework of school autonomy and choice, principals are increasingly obligated to actively market and promote their schools. This shift arises from policies that grant schools more control over their operations while introducing competitive elements similar to those in the private sector. As a result, principals must emphasise their school's unique strengths and achievements to attract and retain students. This involves creating compelling narratives about the school's educational quality, extracurricular offerings, and overall environment to stand out from other schools in the area. In Victoria, schools are encouraged to use public funds for marketing efforts, such as installing billboards, developing marketing images, and creating electronic name boards and other promotional materials to enhance their visibility and appeal.

Bringing Local Actors into the Decision-Making

School autonomy decentralises decision-making, involving various local stakeholders in financial matters, granting them direct access to funds. Particularly in remote areas, schools serve as significant local entities, assuming responsibility for financial management and decision-making, albeit transferring it to a group of unpredictable local actors. However, mobilising resources without proper oversight poses risks, including financial irregularities and inefficient resource allocation, emphasising the need for local capability, accountability, and control mechanisms.

Empowering schools with greater decision-making authority often involves input from diverse stakeholders such as teachers, parents, students, and community members, each contributing unique perspectives and priorities. While this diversity enriches decision-making, it also introduces complexity and necessitates negotiations to balance competing interests and ensure consensus. Principals must navigate these complexities transparently, fostering collaboration while adhering to legal and regulatory standards to address potential conflicts and disagreements.

Creating Uneasy Partnerships

School autonomy often leads to uneasy partnerships, particularly when parents or laymen become involved in the decision-making processes of professional entities. Principals and teachers, as professionals, adhere to long-standing traditions, values, and operational practices. They possess specialised knowledge and skills acquired through education and training, enabling them to fulfill their roles effectively. On the other hand, parents and community members, coming from diverse backgrounds with their own vested interests, may be unsure about their roles within the school governance structure.

This dynamic can create tensions and strained relationships between school principals and school councils. While the role of a school council in Victoria is primarily to establish long-term goals for the school and oversee its operations, it does not involve day-to-day management, which falls under the purview of the school principal. However, some school councils may either underperform or merely serve as a rubber stamp, allowing local bureaucrats to exert undue influence.

Misunderstandings or misconceptions about respective roles can lead to inefficiencies and create an uneasy environment for governance, ultimately eroding solidarity within the school community. School professionals must navigate these challenges while also managing local conditions, striking the right balance, and effectively handling the complexities of these partnerships.

Altering Professional Identity

Policies in Victoria under neoliberal framework significantly alter the professional identity of school principals by placing a strong emphasis on market-oriented practices rather than traditional educational values. These policies promote a competitive, performance-driven approach where the success of schools is often measured by metrics such as standardised test scores, graduation rates, and other quantifiable outcomes. As a result, principals are compelled to adopt strategies akin to those used in the business world, focusing on efficiency, accountability, and consumer satisfaction. This shift prioritises the economic aspects of education, such as cost-effectiveness and market competitiveness, over the intrinsic educational goals of fostering critical thinking, creativity, and holistic development in students. Consequently, principals may find themselves balancing the pressures of meeting external performance benchmarks while trying to uphold the educational mission and values of their schools. This redefinition of their roles can lead to a professional identity crisis, where principals might struggle to maintain their commitment to educational ideals in the face of mounting demands to operate their schools more like businesses. This tension can impact their job satisfaction, professional fulfillment, and ultimately the educational experiences of the students they serve.

Diminishing Autonomy

Neoliberal reforms, characterised by their emphasis on market principles and accountability, can also significantly reduce the autonomy of school principals by imposing rigid performance standards and accountability frameworks. These reforms often entail a top-down approach where principals are required to adhere strictly to standardised metrics for evaluating school performance, such as test scores, graduation rates, and other quantifiable indicators.

The focus on measurable outcomes leaves little room for principals to exercise professional discretion or innovate in response to the unique needs and contexts of their schools. Instead of acting as autonomous educational leaders who can tailor their strategies to foster holistic student development and community engagement, principals become enforcers of externally imposed benchmarks. This constraint not only limits their ability to implement creative and context-specific educational practices but also stifles their professional judgment and leadership capabilities.

The pressure to comply with these inflexible standards can lead to a narrowed vision of educational success, prioritising compliance over genuine educational improvement. Consequently, the diminished autonomy undermines principals' capacity to act as transformative leaders who can inspire and cultivate meaningful educational experiences, affecting their sense of efficacy and satisfaction in their roles.

Challenges for School Principals

High Demand on Educational Leadership

As already highlighted, the demand for educational leadership in devolved governance systems is substantial. Educational leadership is not a skill that can be easily imparted through training; rather, it is a quality inherent in individuals who possess empathy, passion, and an unwavering dedication to enriching the lives of students. Effective educational leaders exemplify ethical behavior, maintaining moral integrity and upholding high ethical standards. Their personal integrity serves as an invisible guiding force, shaping the cultural ethos of the school and driving educational performance.

Principals who demonstrate integrity and commitment play a pivotal role in inspiring teachers and fostering a culture of excellence. Their leadership creates a supportive environment that empowers teachers to navigate local challenges and achieve educational goals. In this context, traditional metrics of school leadership take a backseat to the intangible qualities of educational leadership.

Shift Towards Managerial Roles

Under neoliberal education policies, school principals are increasingly viewed as managers rather than educational leaders, with a primary focus on efficiency, budget management, and performance outcomes. This shift emphasises the operational aspects of running a school, where principals are expected to maximise resource utilisation, adhere to strict budgetary constraints, and meet performance targets often measured by standardised testing and other quantitative metrics. As a result, the traditional role of principals as pedagogical leaders, who inspire and support teaching and learning, is overshadowed by managerial responsibilities that align more closely with corporate practices. This redefinition of their role can lead to a narrowing of their focus, prioritising measurable outputs over the broader educational mission of fostering a holistic and enriching learning environment for students. This managerial approach often necessitates the adoption of business-like strategies within schools, potentially at the expense of the relational and developmental aspects of educational leadership that are crucial for creating supportive and nurturing school communities.

Manage Local Educational Needs Locally

The demand to address local educational needs at the grassroots level is amplified by school autonomy and devolution. In this decentralised environment, there is a call to identify, diagnose, and tackle local educational challenges through tailored solutions. This entails recognising the unique needs of each community, formulating localised plans and strategies, mobilising local resources, enhancing local capacity, fostering partnerships within the community, and securing financial support for essential programs and initiatives.

Particularly in areas where parents do not have the option to choose among multiple schools, government schools serve as the sole formal educational institution. Consequently, it becomes imperative for these schools to cater to the educational needs of local children.

The Education and Training Reform Act 2006 underscores the principle of equitable access to quality education for all Victorians, regardless of their location or socioeconomic status. This legislation emphasises the importance of nurturing a lifelong passion for learning and maximising individual potential. As such, school principals and councils bear the significant responsibility of devising localised strategies to address educational challenges within their respective communities, navigating diverse circumstances to ensure the fulfillment of this mandate.

Work Intensification and Administration Burden

Devolution necessitates self-managing schools, significantly increasing the administrative burdens on principals who must now manage beyond educational leadership. In Victoria, central funds are directly allocated to schools, granting them management authority. School councils ensure accountability for public resources. Consequently, principals oversee teaching, manage operations, and handle complex administrative duties mandated by central authorities. They spend significant time on purchasing decisions, budgeting, financial management, implementing internal controls, and monitoring financial performance. These tasks demand technical expertise and business acumen, adding complexity to their roles.

Neoliberal education policies further intensify principals' workload, requiring continuous improvement and stringent accountability measures. Principals must consistently monitor school performance, implement new initiatives, and comply with extensive reporting standards. This relentless drive for measurable outcomes often leads to long working hours, heavy administrative loads, and pressure to meet performance targets, overshadowing their educational leadership duties. The resulting stress reduces time for meaningful interactions with students, teachers, and the community, eroding work-life balance and job satisfaction. The continuous pressure strains their personal lives and professional identity, impacting their well-being and effectiveness as leaders. This highlights the need for a balanced approach that recognises the multifaceted role of principals, ensuring they can fulfill both managerial and educational responsibilities effectively.

Tendencies Towards Routines and Vulnerabilities Among School Principals

School principals, granted autonomy, may fall into routines and complacency, risking stagnation and inefficiency. While stability is vital, they must remain vigilant to community signals and educational trends to ensure effectiveness. Autonomy can lead to isolation, detaching principals from collaborative networks and external feedback. To counter these tendencies, principals should cultivate habits of revitalisation and continuous supervision, consistently oversee financial management, and update practices. Staying informed about new methodologies and engaging in professional development fosters a dynamic environment. Trust in staff is essential, but supplementary controls and seeking feedback enhance accountability. Collaborating with colleagues, addressing conflicts transparently, and maintaining integrity help principals navigate challenges effectively, maintaining trust within the school community.

Teachers

Changing Role of Teachers

Neoliberal education policies have profoundly transformed the role of teachers, shifting from traditional educators to multi-faceted professionals tasked with meeting stringent performance metrics. Traditionally, teachers focused on holistic student development, emphasising creativity, critical thinking, and individualised attention. However, the neoliberal emphasis on accountability has redefined their role, requiring them to prioritise standardised testing and data-driven results. This shift has increased administrative duties and pressures to perform, often at the expense of educational breadth and depth. Teachers now spend significant time on bureaucratic tasks, such as data recording and compliance with accountability standards, which detracts from their capacity to engage deeply with students. This paradigm shift not only undermines teachers' professional autonomy but also leads to job insecurity and increased stress, fundamentally altering their traditional role as dedicated educators committed to nurturing and inspiring students. Further analysis captured in the next chapter.

School Councils

Challenges for School Councils

School councils face significant challenges with increased governance and accountability requirements. With devolved authority, they are responsible for major financial and operational decisions, often without adequate training or support. Council members, typically volunteers, must meet stringent accountability standards, manage budgets, oversee procurement processes, and ensure compliance with regulatory frameworks. This can be overwhelming and lead to a reliance on principals and business managers, potentially reducing the council's effectiveness in providing genuine community oversight and input.

Despite these challenges, school councils remain crucial forums for community members to exchange information, share experiences, and develop a shared vision for children's education. Councils require members who are genuinely interested in education and willing to contribute. Effective councils ensure active involvement in decision-making, respect for opposing views, and cooperation. They navigate competing ideologies and power struggles while making informed decisions about resource use and ensuring accountability. Conflicts should be managed through partnership, dialogue, and compromise. Ultimately, school councils bridge the gap between parents and teachers, fostering partnerships and solidarity in children's education.

Creating a functional and effective governance structure within schools, particularly in a decentralised environment, can be a mammoth task for community-led school councils. This requires ongoing support and capacity-building efforts to ensure that all members are well-equipped to contribute effectively to school governance. Such support is essential for maintaining a dynamic and responsive school environment that balances operational efficiency with the educational mission of fostering student growth and development.

Chapter 21

Devolution Paradox: Trends of Bureaucratisation of School Leadership in Victoria

Introduction

This chapter examines the potential impact of school autonomy on undermining school-level educational leadership in the teaching and learning process.

Schools as Loosely Coupled Systems

Educational institutions like schools are often regarded as loosely coupled systems that facilitate the teaching and learning process with minimal central control. The classroom serves as the focal point, where teachers directly engage with students to impart knowledge and skills. Educational leadership and incentives typically come from the principal, who interacts with the available resources and support mechanisms and enhance support to teachers without teachers' direct involvement (refers to Figure 9).

Teaching and learning encompass a psychological process involving the interaction between teachers and students, integrating cognitive, emotional, and behavioural aspects to acquire knowledge and skills. Teaching requires instructors' deliberate efforts to convey information, foster understanding, and develop skills through various strategies like explanation, questioning, and feedback. These dynamic processes occur within institutional contexts like school and classroom environments, informing effective instructional practices and enhancing student engagement.

Figure 9: Core Teaching & Learning Process

```
                    Resources and
                       Support

              Core
          Teaching &
           Learning
            Process


                    Educational Leadership
                         by Principal
```

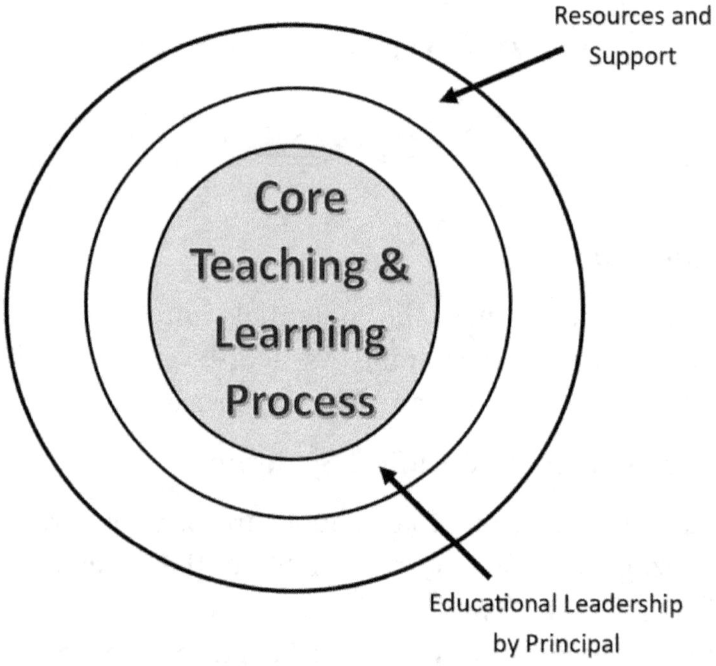

Loosely coupled systems in educational organisations possess several distinguishing characteristics, as outlined by Karl E. Weick (1976). They are dynamic, allowing elements within the organisation to adapt and change in response to various needs and conditions. Flexibility and adaptability are inherent traits, enabling ties between components to accommodate shifting circumstances. Uncertainty in teaching methods and spontaneous mechanisms further enhances their flexibility, shaping their connections and bonds.

Classrooms exemplify loosely coupled systems, where teachers and students operate somewhat independently yet maintain coherence within the larger organisational context. This local setup enables diverse teaching approaches, localised decision-making, and flexibility to address individual student needs. With limited central control, classrooms and educational institutions function independently. The teaching and learning process, along with organisational culture, significantly influence educational performance outcomes. It can be interpreted that schools and classrooms can operate independently for the benefit of the students with minimal intervention and control mechanisms from the centre. Centralised reform efforts run the risk of losing effectiveness or relevance in the classroom learning environment and may even prove counterproductive overall if they fail to grasp local realities.

Impact of Neoliberal Policies on Teachers

Neoliberal economic and education policies have impacted teachers, affecting various aspects of their professional lives and the educational landscape. One significant consequence is the increased emphasis on accountability and performance metrics. According to Ball (2003), teachers are frequently evaluated based on student test scores and other standardised measures of academic achievement. This emphasis can lead to heightened stress and pressure, as job security and professional evaluations become closely tied to student outcomes. Moreover, this focus on performance metrics often narrows the curriculum, as teachers prioritise test preparation over a broader educational experience (Apple, 2004).

These policies also contribute to the intensification of teachers' work. As noted by Day and Smethem (2009), teachers face increased administrative tasks, data recording, and reporting requirements, often without corresponding increases in pay or resources. This intensification results in longer working hours as teachers strive to meet the demands of paperwork, planning, and accountability standards. The added pressures and workload can lead to higher levels of burnout and job dissatisfaction among educators (Hargreaves, 2003). Furthermore, the erosion of professional autonomy undermines teachers' ability to exercise their professional judgment, which is crucial for creative and individualised teaching approaches (Sachs, 2001).

The marketisation and privatisation trends within neoliberal policies introduce further challenges. The introduction of market mechanisms, such as school choice and competition among schools, can lead to job insecurity and a shift in focus from educational quality to profit-making (Hursh, 2007). Schools may prioritise marketing and attracting students over genuine educational improvements, altering the nature of teachers' roles. Additionally, underfunding resulting from cost-cutting measures can exacerbate inequities, creating disparities in working conditions and resources available to teachers (Lipman, 2011). Overall, while neoliberal policies aim to enhance efficiency and accountability, they often lead to unintended negative consequences such as teacher burnout, job insecurity, and a narrowing of educational objectives, highlighting the need for policies that support and empower teachers (Connell, 2013).

Skills and Professional Standards

As mentioned elsewhere, teachers and principals are professionals with unique sets of knowledge, skills, and training. They have professional standards and licensing and certification to practice in education.

Central officials typically have responsibilities to involve in policy development, budget management, program oversight, and enforce regulatory compliance at a broader level. While they may not have backgrounds working as teachers or principals, or knowledge about school teaching and learning environments, they often rely on input from educators, school leaders, and education experts to inform their decision-making invariably.

Figure 10: Demands on School Principals

In Australia, education policymaking and administration at the central level can be performed by officials with expertise from business administration, accounting, legal practice, and economics, mainly because educational administration is regarded as running a business, and mainly business knowledge and experience is valued. Even new business graduates who join the public service may develop policies and guidelines for professionals like school principals without understanding complexity and magnitude of their role. Although feedback on policies is obtained, it is possible that the original idea can remain and the underlying theory may not be practicable to education.

Once policies are developed, they must be implemented and adhered to, with any deviation considered non-compliance, failure, or misconduct. Although principals possess the academic freedom and right to criticise policy and protest, such actions are infrequent. Principals often perceive this as an unnecessary time commitment that can impact on the core aspects of education. Consequently, they may choose to comply rather than contest what they view as a futile exercise. Under such circumstances, symbolic compliance can arise, where actual practices become detached from compliance requirements.

Education policymakers in Finland, for example, often have experience as teachers or principals. This emphasis on educational expertise is reflected in Finland's education system and performance, which is highly regarded internationally.

Influx of New Managerial and Corporate Values into School Administration

School autonomy can theoretically bring fresh perspectives and innovative approaches to school administration. It allows schools to tailor their management practices to their unique needs and challenges, fostering creativity and adaptability. This can lead to the adoption of more efficient and effective managerial practices, improving overall school performance.

However, autonomy may also lead to the introduction of managerial and corporate values that prioritise bureaucratic processes, undermining educational outcomes. In some cases, increased autonomy may result in a focus on administrative tasks rather than educational leadership, leading to a disconnection between managerial decisions and the needs of students and teachers.

School choice and school autonomy tend to bring out and infuse new principles of management into education administration, which are based on private sector values of efficiency and productivity. The achievement of financial and other targets becomes a priority. This new trend transforms the ethical change in governance from the traditional principle of public welfare to the commercial norm of value-for-money. Lynch (2014) suggests that this shift moves from citizens, rights, welfare, and solidarity to customers, service users, and competition. The focus is on the outputs that can be achieved through better monitoring of employee performance, widespread use of performance indicators, league tables, target setting, and benchmarking.

It is acknowledged that managing a school calls for many skills. Some skills are technical, such as planning, budgeting, time management, and monitoring. However, there are unique challenges in education that are not valued by corporate culture. These challenges include developmental and nurturing skills required to enable students to grow and develop (Lynch, 2014). School leaders' support is necessary for teachers to fulfill that task.

There is an emotional investment in people that is not required in private sector organisations, as the product in education is the development and care of others. Managerial concepts originated in a commercial context where process is subordinated to output and profit. Nurturing learners has an outcome dimension, and gains are not measured in a narrowly specified time frame. Even caring could be monitored and measured through matrices that should not undermine the very principle of relatedness and maturity which is at the heart of teaching and learning (Lynch, Grummell, and Devine, 2012).

New managerialism can polarise leaders in education from those who care for student welfare and development to those whose focus is more on products, efficiency gains, performance indicators, and the deployment of a jungle of tools residing in corporate terminology.

It is reasonable to accept that the environment in education management is evolving. However, there is a risk that genuine school leaders who commit their life to nurturing, caring, and educating our kids under difficult circumstances can miss out as far as recognition, advancement, and reward are concerned. Managerialism can present more weaknesses than strengths when applied to educational administration.

Devolution Paradox

The devolution paradox in educational governance describes how efforts to decentralise decision-making authority and promote local autonomy often paradoxically led to increased centralisation of power and control (Rodríguez-Pose, & Gill, 2003; Brenner, 2004).

This paradox becomes evident when devolved governance structures, intended to empower local stakeholders like schools, end up reinforcing central control through mechanisms like strict guidelines, regulations, and compliance requirements.

Despite the aim of decentralisation, several factors contribute to this paradox. Firstly, devolution initiatives tend to bring heightened demands for standardisation and accountability. Requirements for standardised assessments and performance metrics, can impose uniformity across schools, centralising educational practices and priorities. Central agencies often retain significant authority over budgetary decisions, limiting the discretion of local stakeholders. Additionally, central authorities frequently maintain influence over educational policy formulation and implementation, shaping the decisions and practices of local actors. Devolution may also exacerbate fragmentation and inequality within education systems. Variations in local capacity and resources can lead to disparities in outcomes, prompting calls for central intervention to address inequities.

Decentralised units may experience simultaneous attempts to centralise power by emphasising central activities like strategic planning, policy development, and performance monitoring. This creates a new layer of bureaucratic control at the centre, diverting resources and attention from local service delivery.

When incidents occur in sensitive areas like integrity, the senior leadership can become anxious. The immediate response from the central bureaucracy often involves developing and implementing system-wide policies, processes, and regulations to eliminate these issues entirely.

These policies can be large-scale, system-wide, overemphasised, and disproportionate until they fully satisfy senior officials. All educational leaders in schools are then required to engage with aspects of the problem area that may not be directly relevant to them or their environment.

While some decision-making processes may improve under decentralisation, the rise of central bureaucracy and formal requirements can lead to a misallocation of time and resources. Central authorities may respond to negative developments by introducing more managerial methods, further solidifying their central positions and interests. Achieving a balance between central control and decentralised authority is crucial for favourable outcomes.

Part VII

Outcomes
Challenges, Learnings & Prospects

Chapter 22

Advocating Fairness: Socio-Political Dynamics Shaping the National Agendas for Power Balance in Education

Introduction

This chapter examines the socio-political dynamics, including lobbying efforts, that continuously shape national agendas influencing school funding and governance policies. These dynamics are characterised by their intensity, with passionate engagement from both proponents and opponents. The influence of these forces plays a crucial role in determining the balance of power. Identifying these national socio-political forces is essential for understanding their ongoing impact on educational policy and power dynamics.

Lobbying.

Lobbying in Australia is a significant and influential aspect of the socio-political landscape for maintaining power balance. Various interest groups, including non-governmental organisations, and advocacy groups, corporations, industry associations, actively engage in lobbying to influence public policy, legislation, and government decisions. Lobbyists often have direct access to politicians, ministers, and senior bureaucrats. They typically have deep knowledge and expertise in specific areas, enabling them to effectively advocate for their positions.

Lobbying groups often run public awareness and advocacy campaigns to sway public opinion and put pressure on politicians. Many lobbying organisations fund or conduct research to support their positions, influencing public policy debates and providing a basis for legislative changes. Governments often engage with various stakeholders, including lobbyists, during consultation processes for policy development. The various agendas of these lobbying groups enrich Australian social democracy by representing diverse viewpoints and interests.

Agenda for Education as Human Rights

Education is recognised as a fundamental human right under various international human rights instruments, despite the absence of a specific UN charter solely dedicated to this right. The Universal Declaration of Human Rights (UDHR) underscores this principle in Article 26, stating that "everyone has the right to education." Similarly, the International Covenant on Economic, Social and Cultural Rights (ICESCR) and the Convention on the Rights of the Child (CRC) affirm the right to education in their respective articles.

These instruments stress the importance of providing education that is accessible, equitable, and of high quality. They emphasise the necessity of free, compulsory primary education and the progressive provision of secondary and higher education. Moreover, Goal 4 of the Sustainable Development Goals (SDGs) highlights the international community's commitment to ensuring inclusive and equitable education for all.

While the UDHR does not specifically address school funding and governance, its principles can inform discussions on these topics. For instance, Article 1 emphasises equality, supporting the equitable distribution of resources in education to ensure equal access for all individuals. Article 21 advocates for stakeholder participation in governance, including parents, teachers, and community members, in decision-making processes related to school funding and resource allocation.

International human rights instruments provide a robust framework for advocating and advancing the right to education globally. They emphasise the importance of equitable access to education and transparent governance processes in educational institutions. By invoking these widely accepted principles, activists can make compelling arguments for equitable school funding and effective governance based on international human rights standards.

Human Rights Advocacy Groups

Lobbying groups such as Amnesty International Australia, Children and Young People with Disability Australia (CYDA), Indigenous Education Consultative Bodies (IECBs), Anglicare Australia, The Smith Family, Brotherhood of St Laurence, and the Australian Human Rights Commission (AHRC) use various methods, including policy advocacy, public campaigns, research, and direct support programs, to promote education as a human right and ensure that all individuals in Australia have access to quality education.

Agenda for Government Schools as the Primary Provider

The non-government school sector in Australia is experiencing growth alongside the increasing momentum of neoliberalist education policies. Despite this trend, the argument for government responsibility in education remains strong. Both liberal and labour forces universally recognise the commitment to government funding for both government and non-government schools due to contextual historical developments.

One argument for running only government schools stems from principles of equity, social cohesion, and the provision of quality education as a public good. Government schools, financed by public resources, ensure equitable access to education for all students, regardless of their socio-economic background or ability to pay. This approach mitigates disparities and fosters social mobility by offering a common educational experience accessible to all.

Moreover, government schools serve as vital community hubs, fostering social cohesion, integration, and a sense of belonging within communities. By providing a shared educational environment, government schools contribute to the development of inclusive and supportive learning environments that benefit all students.

Recognised widely as a public good benefiting society, education in government schools prioritises the delivery of quality education over profit motives. Operated and funded by the state, government schools prioritise collective well-being and educational outcomes, rather than catering to individual interests or market demands.

Government schools operate under democratic governance structures, subject to public oversight and accountability mechanisms. This ensures transparency, accountability, and democratic decision-making in education policy and practice, upholding democratic values and reflecting the needs and interests of the broader public.

Consolidating resources within a single public education system leads to more efficient allocation of resources and economies of scale. By eliminating duplication and streamlining administrative processes, the education system maximises the impact of public funding and resources, directing them towards improving teaching and learning outcomes for all students.

In contrast, Finland's decision to predominantly have public schools is influenced by historical, cultural, and educational principles. Equity and equality are central to Finnish educational values, aiming to reduce educational disparities and foster social cohesion. Trust in public institutions, a focus on teacher professionalism, and a view of education as a public investment further shape Finland's approach to education, contributing to its reputation for educational excellence.

Common misconceptions about government funding to government schools include the belief that it is a waste of taxpayer money. In reality, such funds are an investment in the nation's future, benefiting individuals, communities, and the country as a whole. Another misconception is that government schools already receive sufficient funding. While they do receive funding, adequate resources are essential to meet the diverse needs of students and provide quality education, promoting equal opportunities and addressing educational disadvantage.

Advocacy for Public Education

Organisations and groups such as the Australian Education Union (AEU), Defence of Government Schools (DOGS), Save Our Schools (SOS), Australian Council of State School Organisations (ACSSO), Public Education Foundation, community and parent groups, teachers and principals, and the Australian Human Rights Commission (AHRC) engage in various activities, including lobbying, public campaigns, research, and direct action, to advocate for stronger support and funding for public education in Australia.

Agenda for Government Funding to Non-Government Schools in Australia

Chubb and Moe (1990) revitalised Friedman's (1982, 1962) earlier contention that an education system driven by market forces, where parents wield primary control over schools, would yield superior outcomes compared to a state-driven approach. They advocated for empowering consumers (students and parents) while reducing state intervention, positing that this would enhance academic achievement and foster greater efficiency and fairness within schools. This perspective, rooted in Milton Friedman's original concept in "Capitalism and Freedom," (1962) suggests that the government's role should be limited to ensuring schools meet basic standards, similar to its oversight of restaurant hygiene.

It was claimed that school choice advocates parental rights to choose as a human right to enable parents to guarantee the best education for their children and to improve the equality of opportunities, thus enabling disadvantaged pupils to visit a 'good school' too (Musset, 2012).

Marketisation and privatisation have since reshaped educational landscapes globally, with increased school choice and the expansion of private or charter schools being notable outcomes. These changes have implications for school quality, organisation, teacher professionalism, teaching methodologies, social segregation, and educational equity.

In Australia, the discourse on government funding for non-government schools reflects diverse perspectives on education, equity, and the government's role. Non-government schools, including independent and Catholic institutions, play pivotal roles in serving the diverse student population. Government funding for these schools fosters educational choice and diversity, enabling parents to select environments aligned with their values and children's needs. Many non-government schools have cultural or religious affiliations, preserving families' rights to educate their children according to their beliefs.

Moreover, non-government schools often offer specialised programs fostering academic excellence and innovation. Contrary to misconceptions, government funding for these schools does not detract from resources available to government schools. Additionally, non-government schools serve students from various socio-economic backgrounds, offering scholarships and financial aid to promote inclusivity and social mobility.

The argument that non-government schools can sustain themselves through tuition fees alone overlooks the critical role of government funding in supporting quality education, providing necessary facilities, and accommodating diverse student needs.

Government funding for non-government schools in Australia has been based on promoting educational choice, diversity, and excellence. By recognising the value of these institutions and directing funds toward them, it is argued that all students have access to high-quality education and that the education system benefits from innovation and competition. Dispelling misconceptions surrounding government funding for non-government schools is essential for acknowledging their vital role in the educational landscape.

Advocacy for Non-Government Schools

Lobbying groups advocating for non-government schools include Independent Schools Australia (ISA), National Catholic Education Commission (NCEC), Catholic Education Offices and Commissions, Australian Association of Christian Schools (AACS), Christian Schools Australia (CSA), Association of Heads of Independent Schools of Australia (AHISA), and Association of Independent Schools (AIS). These organisations and activists engage in lobbying, public campaigns, research, and policy advocacy to ensure that Catholic and independent schools receive adequate funding and support from the government. They emphasise the importance of school choice and the role of non-government schools in providing quality education.

Agenda for Sector-Blind Government Funding

The concept of sector-blind funding is referenced in the Gonski Report, which was released in December 2011. The specific reference to sector-blind funding can be found in Chapter 2 of the report, titled "Schooling in Australia." In this chapter, the Gonski panel discusses the principles that should underpin school funding arrangements, including fairness, transparency, and effectiveness.

Sector-blind funding refers to a funding approach in education where financial support is provided to schools without discrimination based on their sector, whether they are government-funded (public) or non-government-funded (private or independent). The Liberal Party of Australia accepts this concept in its party statement and advocates it.

The argument for sector-blind funding in Australia revolves around principles of equity and fairness in education funding. Advocates argue that all schools, regardless of their ownership or governance, should receive funding based on the needs of their students and the costs associated with delivering quality education. They argue that funding should be allocated based on factors such as student demographics, socio-economic status, and educational requirements, rather than the sector of the school.

Proponents of sector-blind funding also argue that it promotes parental choice in education by allowing families to choose the school that best meets their child's needs, regardless of whether it is a government or non-government school. They assert that funding should follow the student, empowering parents to make decisions about their child's education without financial barriers.

However, critics of sector-blind funding raise concerns about the potential for inequities and inefficiencies in the distribution of funding. They argue that prioritising sector-blind funding may result in disproportionate funding allocation to more advantaged schools or exacerbate existing inequalities in the education system. Critics also argue that sector-blind funding fails to address the unique challenges and responsibilities of government schools, which serve a diverse range of students and often cater to disadvantaged communities.

Overall, the debate around sector-blind funding in Australia reflects broader discussions about equity, choice, and the role of government in education funding. Both proponents and critics continue to advocate for policies that ensure fair and equitable funding while addressing the diverse needs of students and schools across different sectors. The Australian Liberal Party is committed to sector-blind funding.

Agenda for Secular Education

The history of secular education in Australia is deeply intertwined with the nation's development, reflecting broader social, political, and cultural shifts over time. Since its inception, secular education, which is education not affiliated with any religious denomination or belief system, has been fundamental to Australia's education system.

During the colonial period, religious institutions primarily provided education in Australia, with denominational schools established by various religious groups such as Anglicans, Catholics, and Presbyterians. These schools often reflected the religious values and teachings of their respective denominations, resulting in a fragmented and sectarian education system.

The momentum for secular education grew in the late 19th and early 20th centuries as Australia moved towards a more unified and democratic society. Secularism emerged as a key principle, advocating for the separation of church and state in education and the establishment of non-sectarian, government-funded schools accessible to all children, regardless of their religious background.

A significant development in secular education history was the introduction of free, compulsory, and secular education legislation in various Australian colonies during the latter half of the 19th century. These laws laid the foundation for state-run public schools that provided education free from religious bias or affiliation.

The passing of the New South Wales Public Schools Act in 1872 marked the beginning of state-funded secular education in Australia, with similar legislation enacted in other colonies, leading to the establishment of public-school systems across the country.

With the federation of Australia in 1901, a national education system was created under the jurisdiction of the federal government. While education policy remained the responsibility of individual states, the federal government played a coordinating role in promoting secular and non-sectarian principles in education.

Throughout the 20th century, secular education continued to evolve and expand in Australia, with the establishment of comprehensive public-school systems that provided education to children from diverse backgrounds and communities. Today, secular education remains fundamental to Australia's education system, with public schools upholding principles of secularism, inclusivity, and diversity.

Secular education in Australia is advocated for on the grounds of fundamental principles such as equality, inclusivity, and the separation of church and state.

Proponents of secular education put forward compelling arguments to support their stance.

Firstly, advocates emphasise the necessity of establishing a neutral learning environment where all students have equal access to education devoid of religious bias or indoctrination. This emphasis on equality and fairness underscores the importance of providing an educational landscape that respects the diverse beliefs and backgrounds of students.

Secondly, proponents assert the importance of maintaining the separation of church and state within the public education system. They argue that public education should remain free from religious influence or control to ensure impartiality and inclusivity, serving the entire community equitably without favouring any particular religious doctrine.

Advocates highlight the significance of religious freedom and contend that secular education plays a crucial role in safeguarding this freedom. By ensuring that religious instruction remains distinct from formal schooling, secular education respects individuals' rights to practice their faith or hold non-religious beliefs without interference from the state.

In addition to these principles, proponents argue that secular schools prioritise academic excellence and equip students with the necessary skills to thrive in a diverse society. By fostering social cohesion through the promotion of universal principles of tolerance, respect, and understanding, secular education contributes to a cohesive and inclusive society where all individuals feel valued and respected. Lastly, advocates express concerns about discrimination in religiously affiliated schools and advocate for secular education as a means to safeguard vulnerable students from discrimination based on their beliefs, background, or identity.

Advocacy Groups for Secular Education

Lobbying groups advocating for secular education in Australia include the Australian Secular Lobby (ASL), Rationalist Society of Australia (RSA), Australian Humanists, Australian Education Union (AEU), Fairness in Religions in Schools (FIRIS), Parents for Secular Schools, Secular Party of Australia, National Secular Lobby (NSL), Public Education Foundation Inc Australia, and Progressive Atheists. These organisations and activists engage in various activities, including lobbying, public awareness campaigns, research, and legal action, to promote secular education in Australia. They aim to ensure that public education remains neutral on religious matters and inclusive of all students, regardless of their religious beliefs or lack thereof.

Historical Campaigns Advocating for Public Education

Save Our Schools (SOS)

Save Our Schools (SOS) is an advocacy organisation in Australia dedicated to promoting equity and fairness within the education system. It was established in July 2006 in response to a proposal by the ACT Labor Government to close 39 public schools and pre-schools and sell-off the sites for development.

One of their primary achievements has been their strong advocacy for equitable funding for public schools. SOS has consistently highlighted the disparities in government funding between public and private schools, pushing for policy changes to ensure that public schools receive adequate resources to meet the educational needs of all students.

SOS is also known for its comprehensive research and reports on school funding, educational inequalities, and the impacts of policy changes on public education. Their data-driven analyses have significantly influenced public discourse and informed policymakers. Furthermore, through media campaigns, public forums, and community engagement, SOS has successfully raised public awareness about the inequities in the education system, mobilising parents, educators, and the general public to advocate for a fairer education system.

The organisation's advocacy efforts have contributed to the national debate on school funding policies, playing a role in shaping discussions around the Gonski reports and the implementation of needs-based funding models. Additionally, SOS has been a vocal supporter of public schools, emphasising their role in providing inclusive and equitable education. They have defended public schools against policies and practices that they perceive as undermining the quality and accessibility of public education.

SOS has also engaged with educational authorities, including the Australian Curriculum, Assessment and Reporting Authority (ACARA), to ensure that the voices of public school advocates are heard in policy-making processes. Overall, Save Our Schools has been instrumental in highlighting and addressing the inequities in Australia's education system, advocating for policies that ensure all students, regardless of their socio-economic background, have access to high-quality education.

Australian Council for the Defence of Government Schools (DOGS)

Robert Menzies won the 1963 federal election partly on the promise of state aid for Catholic schools. In 1964, his government provided federal funding to both public and private schools for science labs and other resources. Teachers' unions and parents formed a lobby group against state aid, called the Australian Council for the Defence of Government Schools (DOGS). It is important to recognise this historically significant and active organisation that lobbies and advocates for the protection and promotion of government schools. DOGS serves as an example of how lobbying groups actively engage in and influence policy changes.

Founded by individuals passionate about protecting government schools, DOGS aimed to advocate for fair and adequate funding to ensure equitable access to quality education for all students. Starting as a grassroots movement, DOGS organised meetings, rallies, and campaigns to raise awareness and challenge funding disparities. Over the years, it has grown in influence, engaging in legal actions, policy discussions, and community outreach to promote the value of government schools.

DOGS plays a crucial role in advocating for the rights and interests of government schools. They work tirelessly to ensure that government schools receive adequate funding, resources, and support to provide quality education to all students. DOGS also raises awareness about the benefits of government schools and challenges misconceptions surrounding their value.

Achievements of DOGS include successful advocacy efforts to raise awareness about the importance of government schools and advocate for increased funding and resources. DOGS has also engaged in legal action to challenge policies and practices that undermine the rights and interests of government schools, ensuring that they receive fair treatment and support. Additionally, DOGS actively engages with the community, organising events, campaigns, and initiatives to promote the value of government schools and encourage public support.

Legal Actions

In addition to their advocacy efforts, DOGS has been involved in various legal actions to promote their cause:

- The DOGS Case (1981): One of the landmark legal cases initiated by DOGS was the DOGS Case in 1981. This case challenged the funding of non-government schools by the Australian government, arguing that it violated the principle of separation of church and state. The High Court of Australia ruled in favour of DOGS, stating that government funding of religious schools was unconstitutional. This decision had a significant impact on the funding landscape of education in Australia.
- The Funding Case (2000): DOGS, along with other education advocacy groups, took legal action against the Australian government's funding policies for non-government schools. They argued that the funding model created inequities and favoured non-government schools over government schools. The case resulted in a significant victory for DOGS, with the Federal Court ruling that the funding policies were discriminatory and

needed to be revised to ensure fair and equitable distribution of resources.

- The Gonski Review and Implementation: DOGS played a crucial role in advocating for the Gonski Review, an independent review of school funding in Australia. The review aimed to address funding inequities and ensure that all schools, including government schools, receive adequate resources. As a result of DOGS' efforts, the Australian government implemented the Gonski funding reforms, which provided additional funding to disadvantaged schools and aimed to improve educational outcomes for all students.
- Challenging Discriminatory Practices: DOGS has also taken legal action to challenge discriminatory practices that undermine the rights and interests of government schools. They have raised concerns about the use of public funding by non-government schools to exclude certain students based on their religious beliefs or other factors. Through their legal initiatives, DOGS aims to ensure that all schools, regardless of their governance, provide equal opportunities and inclusivity for students.

DOGS (Australian Council for Defence of Government Schools) is a vital organisation that advocates for the protection and promotion of government schools in Australia. Through their advocacy efforts, legal actions, and community engagement, DOGS works tirelessly to ensure that government schools receive adequate funding, resources, and support to provide quality education to all students. It is important to recognise the value of government schools and support organisations like DOGS in their mission to defend and support public education in Australia. Today, DOGS remains dedicated to defending and supporting government schools, striving for a fair and equitable education system in Australia.

These agendas and lobbying groups are vibrant and active within the Australian political landscape. Each advocate for fairness and equity from their unique perspectives, sparking passionate debates that influence decision-making. Their efforts contribute significantly to enriching Australia's social democracy.

Chapter 23

Assessing Educational Equity: School Funding Disparities and Unmet Expectations

Introduction

This chapter delves into the assessment of school funding effectiveness by examining indicators related to educational performance and the status of resource allocation in Australia. It explores whether there have been improvements in the country's educational achievements due to funding distribution formulas, as evidenced by assessments like PISA and NAPLAN. Additionally, it examines whether there has been an equal and fair distribution of funds among schools, school sectors, and students, and what consequences have resulted from these funding practices.

Assessing the Effectiveness of School Funding

Evaluating the effectiveness of school funding and governance can be approached through two main groups of indicators. The first group focuses on educational performance, which includes consistent and rising test scores, higher graduation rates, and improved academic performance across all subjects and grades. Effective progress in this area can be marked by both elevated educational achievement levels and the narrowing of achievement gaps among diverse student demographics, such as those defined by socioeconomic status, race, ethnicity, or disability.

The second group of indicators will pertain to resource allocation, such as higher per-pupil funding, better access to educational materials and technology, and a more equitable distribution of qualified teachers and staff. Achieving equity and fairness in this context means ensuring a more balanced distribution of resources among schools and students, aiming to mitigate disparities in educational opportunities and outcomes.

The following section investigates how Australia is progressing in these two broad areas.

Australia's Educational Achievements - PISA

From the 1980s onward, slogans like the 'clever country' (Hawke, 1990) framed education as a matter of international competitiveness. In the twenty-first century, this focus was solidified by the triennial assessments. One area of the indicators that help to understand the educational achievements in Australia since 2013 is the Programme for International Student Assessment (PISA) and Trends in International Mathematics and Science Study (TIMSS). These evaluations benchmark students' proficiency in core subjects such as mathematics, science, and reading literacy, providing a benchmark for comparison with other nations.

The mean performance in mathematics, reading, and science in Australia has shown a declining trend from 2012 to 2022, as indicated by the average 10-year trend in mean performance.

The average 10-year trend in mean performance from 2012 to 2022 shows a decrease of 15 points across mathematics, reading, and science subjects. This downward trend indicates a decline in overall academic performance in these areas over the specified period in Australia.

Figure 11 PISA Performance

Area	2012	2022	Difference
Mathematics	504	487	-17
Reading	512	498	-14
Science	521	507	-14

However, the PISA 2022 results also offer insights into Australia's educational performance vis-à-vis other OECD nations:

- Mathematics Performance: 12% of Australian students achieved Levels 5 or 6 in the PISA mathematics test, surpassing the OECD average of 9%. Australia's mathematics score outpaced the OECD average.
- Reading Performance: 79% of Australian students reached Level 2 or higher in reading, exceeding the OECD average of 74%. Moreover, 12% of Australian students attained Levels 5 or higher in reading, surpassing the OECD average of 7%.
- Science Performance: 80% of Australian students attained Level 2 or higher in science, outstripping the OECD average of 76%. Additionally, 13% of Australian students demonstrated proficiency at Levels 5 or 6 in science, exceeding the OECD average of 7%.

Australia's performance in these assessments has generally remained steady, with students typically scoring around the OECD average. However, concerns have arisen regarding declining performance in certain areas and widening achievement gaps among different student demographics, particularly along socio-economic and geographical lines.

The 2022 OECD Programme for International Student Assessment (PISA) data reveals significant inequities in Australia's school system, particularly in resource allocation between advantaged and disadvantaged schools (Save Our Schools, 2024). The resource gaps in Australia are among the largest in the OECD, with 61% of Australian 15-year-old students reporting their learning hindered by a shortage of teachers, marking a drastic increase from 17% in 2018. This shortage has significantly negatively impacted average student mathematics achievement, contributing to one of the largest declines in the OECD. Additionally, 27% of students experienced learning barriers due to a lack of fully qualified teachers, with this factor also heavily affecting mathematics performance.

Low socio-economic status (SES) schools in Australia are especially disadvantaged, facing greater shortages of educational staff, materials, and digital resources compared to high SES schools. The teacher shortage gap between low and high SES schools was the largest in the OECD in both 2018 and 2022. Similarly, the shortage of educational materials in low SES schools is the fifth largest, and the lack of digital resources for students in these schools is the sixth largest within the OECD. Furthermore, class sizes in low SES schools do not differ significantly from those in high SES schools, unlike in most OECD countries where smaller class sizes in disadvantaged schools are used to address inequalities. Public schools also face greater shortages compared to private schools, with significant gaps in educational staff, materials, and digital resources. Rural schools experience more severe shortages than urban schools, further highlighting the disparities in educational resources across Australia (Save Our Schools, 2024).

Australia's Current Educational Achievements - NAPLAN

Another avenue for assessing educational achievements is the Australia's primary national assessment of student performance, the National Assessment Program Literacy and Numeracy (NAPLAN), which was initiated in 2008 under the Federal Labor Government.

NAPLAN is an annual assessment conducted in Australia for students in Years 3, 5, 7, and 9. It tests essential skills in reading, writing, spelling, grammar, punctuation, and numeracy. NAPLAN is designed to assess the literacy and numeracy skills that are critical for students' success in school and life. NAPLAN results are publicly available on the My School website since its launch in 2010.

Analysing NAPLAN results, the National Minimum Standard (NMS) is the agreed minimum acceptable standard of knowledge and skills that students are expected to achieve at each year level. Students who achieve at or above the NMS are considered to have met the minimum acceptable standard for their year level. On the other hand, students who fall below the NMS may require additional support and intervention to help them attain the necessary skills to progress in their schooling.

While acknowledging that NAPLAN results may be more practical for assessing and comparing individual schools and students, the following table and the commentary provide a brief national outlook.

Figure 12: NAPLAN Results

Domain	Mean Scaled Score (2008)	Mean Scaled Score (2017)	Mean Scaled Score (2022)	% at or above NMS (2008)	% at or above NMS (2017)	% at or above NMS (2022)
Reading Y3	401.2	431.3	437.8	92.8	94.9	95.5
Reading Y5	476.4	505.7	509.7	89.7	93.9	95.0
Reading Y7	534.2	544.7	542.6	93.9	94.0	94.2
Reading Y9	578.8	580.9	577.6	93.0	91.7	89.6
Numeracy Y3	408.9	409.4	399.8	96.9	95.4	95.0
Numeracy Y5	487.8	493.8	488.3	94.4	95.4	95.1
Numeracy Y7	551.3	553.9	546.3	96.0	95.4	92.0
Numeracy Y9	591.4	591.9	584.4	94.7	95.8	95.0

(Source: ACARA, NAPLAN National Report, 2022)

The comparative analysis of NAPLAN results for 2008, 2017, and 2022 reveals trends in student performance in reading and numeracy over the years. Reading scores have generally improved from 2008 to 2022, as evidenced by increases in mean scaled scores and the percentage of students at or above the National Minimum Standard (NMS) across most year levels. Conversely, numeracy scores have fluctuated over the same period, with variations observed in mean scaled scores and the percentage of students meeting or exceeding the

NMS across different year levels, making it difficult to observe consistent and significant improvements.

While these scores are indicative, some influencing factors could be beyond the control of school funding and governance initiatives. Continued monitoring and analysis of NAPLAN results remain crucial for tracking student performance, identifying areas for improvement, and informing targeted strategies to support student learning and achievement.

It appears that there is no observable boost of improvement as expected by school funding and governance arrangements.

Equity and Fairness in Funds Allocation

According to the National Report on Schooling in Australia 2022 produced by ACARA, the total gross recurrent income for all schools in Australia was $80.05 billion, made up of $25.62 billion (32.0%) from Australian Government recurrent funding, $39.98 billion (49.9%) from state/territory government recurrent funding, $12.65 billion (15.8%) from fees, charges, and parent contributions, and $1.81 billion (2.3%) from other private contributions.

Australian Government recurrent funding accounted for 20.7% of the total gross income for government schools, with state and territory governments providing 75.6% of funds. For non-government schools, the Australian Government contributed 60.7% of Catholic sector gross income and 38.3% of independent sector gross income. Income from fees, charges, and parent contributions made up 21.2% of Catholic sector income and 46.9% of independent sector income.

In 2022, average gross recurrent income per student, across all Australian schools, was $19,685. It was higher for independent schools ($25,695) than for Catholic schools ($19,681) and government schools ($18,076).

Figure 13: Disparities in Funds Allocation

School Sector	Recurrent Income per student	Difference + or − from all schools $
Independent	$25,695	+$6,010
Catholic	$19,681	−$4
Government	$18,076	−$1,614
All schools (average)	$19,685	

Federal Minister for Education publicly acknowledged on 26 September 2016 (ABC Q&A) that some private schools are over-funded.

Disparities in Funding

Cobbold (2020) discovered after analysis that between 2009-10 and 2017-18, government funding significantly favoured private schools over public schools in Australia. During this period, government funding for private schools increased by $1,779 per student (adjusted for inflation), whereas funding for public schools was cut by $49 per student. This disparity is further highlighted by the fact that government funding for private schools rose by 18.9%, while funding for public school students decreased by 0.4%.

The Commonwealth Government contributed to this imbalance by increasing funding for both public and private schools, but the increase for private schools was nearly double that for public schools. Specifically, Commonwealth funding for public schools increased by an average of $863 per student, compared to $1,589 for private schools. This trend was consistent across all states, with Commonwealth funding increases heavily favouring private schools in every state.

The overall reduction in funding for public schools was primarily due to significant cuts by state governments, which more than offset the Commonwealth's increases. On average, state government funding for public schools was cut by $912 per student, while private schools saw an increase of $190 per student. Notably, all state governments, regardless of political affiliation, implemented large cuts to public school funding while providing modest increases for private schools during this period.

The latest analysis by Cobbold (March 24, 2024) highlights a significant disparity in government funding increases between private and public schools in Australia since 2009. Data from the Australian Curriculum and Reporting Authority (ACARA, 2024) reveals that funding for Catholic and Independent schools has surged far beyond that of public schools. Specifically, Commonwealth and state government funding boosts for Catholic schools amounted to $2,865 per student, while independent schools saw an increase of $2,500 per student, compared to a mere $1,621 for public schools. This substantial discrepancy in funding growth has led to private schools enjoying a much higher income per student, resulting in a significant resource advantage over public schools. Additionally, the report underscores the growing dependence of private schools on government funding, with Catholic schools relying on government funding for 76% of their income in 2022, up from 72% in 2009, and independent schools increasing their reliance from 41% to 49%. This heightened reliance on government funding by private schools contrasts starkly with the challenges faced by disadvantaged students, the majority of whom attend public schools.

Furthermore, Cobbold sheds light on the widening achievement gaps between high socio-economic status (SES) students and disadvantaged students in reading, mathematics, and science since 2006. The data reveals that the percentage of disadvantaged students not achieving basic proficiency standards is notably higher than that of high SES students, with the achievement gaps between these groups increasing over the years. Given that the majority of low SES, Indigenous, and remote area students are enrolled in public schools, the report underscores the urgent need for equitable funding to address these widening disparities and support the educational needs of disadvantaged students.

It appears that urgent action required to address the under-funding of public schools, which are currently operating at only 87.6% of their Schooling Resource Standard (SRS) in 2024. The estimated funding shortfall of about $6.8 billion highlights the critical need for public schools to be fully funded at 100% of their SRS without any accounting tricks. Cobbold emphasises that improving school outcomes for disadvantaged students hinges on equitable funding allocation and transparent government actions, urging the Commonwealth and State Governments to prioritise genuine full funding for public schools to ensure the future prospects of disadvantaged students and uphold principles of educational equity.

Implications

The substantial difference in average income per student between private and public schools highlights significant resource allocation disparities among school sectors. Private schools, particularly independent ones, benefit from higher incomes per student, allowing them to invest more in facilities, staff, extracurricular activities, and specialised programs. This financial advantage results in a more resource-rich educational environment compared to Catholic and government schools, thereby offering students in private institutions a broader range of opportunities and experiences.

Higher income per student in independent schools often translates into enhanced educational quality, such as smaller class sizes, better-equipped classrooms, and access to advanced technology and enrichment programs. On the other hand, government schools, with their lower income per student, frequently face resource constraints, leading to larger class sizes and fewer specialised programs and extracurricular activities. This disparity raises equity and fairness concerns, as students from lower-income families attending government schools may be at a disadvantage in accessing the same quality of education and opportunities available to their peers in independent schools.

Disparity at the Macro Level

There is substantial evidence indicating that, on average, students in private schools in Australia tend to achieve better academic results compared to their peers in government schools. This is demonstrated through various assessments and studies, including the National Assessment Program - Literacy and Numeracy (NAPLAN), which consistently shows higher average scores for private school students in reading, writing, and numeracy across different year levels. The Programme for International Student Assessment (PISA) results also highlight that Australian private school students achieve higher scores in reading, mathematics, and science. Additionally, state-based senior secondary certificate exams, such as the Higher School Certificate (HSC) in New South Wales and the Victorian Certificate of Education (VCE) in Victoria, reveal that private school students generally achieve higher ATAR scores.

Reports from the Australian Curriculum, Assessment and Reporting Authority (ACARA) further indicate that students in non-government schools achieve better academic outcomes, even when socio-economic factors are considered. Longitudinal studies, such as the Longitudinal Surveys of Australian Youth (LSAY), show that private school students have better academic outcomes and higher university entrance rates. These various sources collectively support the assertion that, on average, students in private schools in Australia achieve better academic results than those in government schools.

However, Government schools enrol a higher percentage of disadvantaged students, including those with disabilities and Indigenous students, leading to disparities in educational achievement across school sectors. This disparity in achievement is further exacerbated by the increasing socio-economic segregation in schools, with higher-income families opting for private schools, contributing to a concentration of advantage in certain sectors and disadvantage in others.

It can identify complexities of fund distribution among different school sectors, pointing out the historical context of government subsidies to private schools and the evolution of funding policies over the years. While there have been policy interventions to address equity in funding allocation, the system remains obscure and inconsistent, with ongoing debates over the fair distribution of federal funds to schools. This disparity in fund distribution has implications for the quality of education provided in different sectors, with some disadvantaged public schools facing resource constraints compared to more advantaged private schools, perpetuating inequalities in the education system.

Moreover, there are challenges of measuring need and entitlement in fund allocation, with promises made to ensure no private school is worse off. The complexities of funding arrangements and the lack of transparency in the distribution of funds raise questions about the effectiveness of current policies in promoting equitable educational outcomes for all students. These disparities in educational achievement and fund distribution underscore the need for comprehensive reforms to address equity issues and ensure a fair and inclusive education system that provides equal opportunities for all students, regardless of their socio-economic background or school sector.

Educational Disadvantage Among Aboriginal and Torres Strait Islander Students

The 2022 National Report on Schooling in Australia underscores the educational performance and challenges faced by Aboriginal and Torres Strait Islander students within the framework of the Closing the Gap Initiative. This initiative seeks to improve education outcomes for

Indigenous students through specific targets aimed at increasing early childhood education enrollment, enhancing developmental outcomes, and achieving higher attainment levels for qualifications and employment. The Australian Government is committed to these goals, emphasising improvements in early education enrollment and developmental outcomes.

However, despite these efforts, the apparent retention rate from Year 10 to Year 12 for Indigenous students declined in 2022 across various regions. The gap in retention rates between Indigenous and non-Indigenous students, influenced by factors such as population size, identification changes, and mobility, remained significant at 24.0 percentage points in 2022, reflecting ongoing challenges in achieving educational parity.

Attendance rates for Aboriginal and Torres Strait Islander students also decreased between 2021 and 2022, further widening the gap compared to non-Indigenous students, especially in remote and very remote areas. Indigenous students consistently showed lower attendance rates than their non-Indigenous peers, with significant disparities in states like the Northern Territory, Western Australia, and South Australia. Additionally, Indigenous students are underrepresented in senior secondary years, predominantly attending government schools. Despite concerted efforts to improve retention, attendance, and enrollment patterns for Indigenous students, substantial challenges and disparities persist. The report highlights the enduring inequities faced by Aboriginal and Torres Strait Islander students in the Australian education system, underscoring the need for continued and intensified efforts to close these educational gaps.

The Closing the Gap initiative faces criticism regarding its policy focus, as highlighted by Mundine (2024). He points out significant disparities between Indigenous communities based on their location. Remote communities experience higher rates of neighbourhood problems compared to urban areas. For example, family violence occurs at a rate of 30% in remote areas, which is four times higher than in urban settings. Additionally, issues such as alcohol consumption, drug use, and children not attending school are more prevalent in remote communities.

Overall, life in remote Indigenous communities is reported to be more than twice as challenging as in urban Indigenous communities across various measures of dysfunction. These disparities underscore the need to tailor policies and programs to address the unique challenges faced by Indigenous communities based on their location to effectively close the gap.

The ongoing debates regarding fair resource distribution are highlighted by the discrepancies in funding allocations between private and government schools. This chapter emphasises the crucial need to address these inequities in both school funding and governance to establish a fair and inclusive education system that benefits all students across Australia.

Chapter 24

Beyond the Norm: Uncovering the Key Drivers and Missing Links Shaping Modern Educational Performance

Introduction

This chapter acknowledges that numerous factors and mechanisms influence educational performance beyond school finance and governance. Several key influences have been presented. In Victoria, multiple pathways to both success and failure are identified, with socio-economic status and student attitudes being significant factors. Additionally, natural progression through lifelong learning has been recognised. The potential role of modern technology-based education, supported by AI, in revolutionising future education delivery is also highlighted. Finally, Australia's strong performance in the international Human Development Index, reflecting its socio-economic prosperity, is noted as an underlying factor advancing education beyond the deliberate efforts of policy changes.

Beyond the Focus of this Publication

This book primarily delves into school finance and governance agenda. It is important to emphasise that myriad other factors, mechanisms, and pathways influence educational performance beyond the scope of this book.

The factors that influence educational performance encompass student attributes, teacher practices, school environment, family and community dynamics, and fast-growing technological advancement. Notable among these are school-related variables, socio-economic background, cultural capital of the home (e.g., parental education level), student cognitive abilities. Peer effects and household location are also considered, with an increased focus on equity funding to address educational disparities.

Hattie (2009) examined six broad areas impacting student learning: the student, the home, the school, the curriculum, the teacher, and teaching and learning strategies, ranking influential aspects within each by their effect sizes. Notably, Hattie emphasised the significant impact of teaching quality on student achievement. The Coleman Report, dating back six decades in the US, suggested that family influences outweigh school funding in affecting achievement scores (Coleman, 1966). Recent empirical evidence identifies various conditions contributing to educational and occupational attainment, as well as social mobility.

Socio-economic status remains the strongest predictor of educational achievement (Miller & Voon, 2011). The Centre for the Study of Higher Education (2008) reveals that individuals from low socio-economic backgrounds are approximately one-third as likely as those from higher socio-economic backgrounds to participate in higher education. Further, Frenette (2007) concludes that economically disadvantaged students in Canada are less likely to pursue a university education than students from affluent families. Moreover, students from well-to-do families are more likely to attend high schools with a higher propensity to produce university-bound students (Frenette, 2007). Finnie and Mueller (2008) also found that in Canada, parental education, not parental income, largely drives young people to attend post-secondary education. However, in the US, attendance is more strongly related to parental income (Belley, Frenette & Lochner, 2011).

Bourdieu argues that parents endow their children with physical, human, social, and particularly "cultural capital," whose transmission creates inequalities in children's educational and occupational attainment (Bourdieu, 1973; Bourdieu & Passeron, 1977). Lareau's research (2002, 2011) discloses important differences in the "cultural tool kit" that families from different class backgrounds wield in their interactions with teachers and schools, and how these differences can translate into contrasting educational trajectories. Inequalities tend to incline toward intergenerational transmission (Farkas, 2003; Edgerton & Roberts, 2014).

The literature on peer effects and social interaction in schooling has grown rapidly (e.g., Hanushek et al., 2003; Angrist & Lang, 2004). It is argued that the social interaction between high- and low-ability students results in positive peer effects and achievement growth. Diverse classrooms may be more efficient because less gifted students benefit from social interaction with high-ability peers (Meier, 2004; Hanushek & Wossman, 2006). However, Gibbons and Telhaj

(2012) question the notion that children benefit from being educated alongside high-ability peers, noting that the magnitude of school-level peer effects is small.

There is ongoing debate about the impact of increased school funding on education since the Coleman Report in 1966. The Gonski Panel (2011) noted five significant factors of disadvantage impacting educational outcomes in Australia: socio-economic status, indigeneity, English language proficiency, disability at the student level, and remoteness at the school level. The Gonski Panel recommended a national needs-based and sector-blind school funding model to ensure equitable educational outcomes. However, Hanushek (2013) questions the impact of additional funding on school performance, arguing that simply providing extra resources to schools without targeting funding to incentives is insufficient to expect higher student achievement.

Paths to Success or Failure.

Analysing the polarisation of high achievement and low achievers in Victoria, the author (Bandaranayake, 2016) found that there is no single factor that determines high or low VCE performance, but rather multiple pathways and causal relations that lead to school success or failure. Three pathways to success and nearly twice as many to failure were identified, with the negative pathways not being mere opposites of the positive ones, highlighting the complexity of the issue. Low socio-economic status often predicts low performance, yet some schools with low ICSEA still achieve success. Factors such as socio-economic status, student attitudes, and metropolitan location influence outcomes, though no single factor is sufficient alone. Despite equity funding through the SRP, persistent educational inequalities remain, suggesting current funding levels and strategies are inadequate. Similar results have been shown in other studies (Caves, et. al. 2015).

The Author's study suggests that while increased funding can potentially be effective, it must be directed towards pragmatic initiatives and teacher-based incentives. It also points out that conditions leading to school failure often persist beyond the control of the schools themselves, indicating that new policy interventions based on causal realities are needed to address inequality. Victoria's alternative educational pathways, such as VET and VCAL, provide options for non-academic students, but socio-economic disparities in higher education participation persist. The study calls for further research to understand the complex causal factors contributing to educational inequality and to develop measures to prevent polarisation and close educational gaps.

Natural Progression

This publication acknowledges that improvements in educational outcomes can also arise from natural progression—the inherent process of education regardless of government intervention. Such progression encompasses individuals' pursuit of knowledge and skills through informal learning, apprenticeships, mentorships, self-study, and community-based education. The journey of lifelong learning entails continually acquiring knowledge and skills to adapt to changing circumstances, pursue personal interests, and advance professional growth. Moreover, fostering intellectual curiosity, encouraging debate, and promoting a renaissance of knowledge can inspire educational motivation and enhance outcomes. Although government interventions may influence certain aspects of education, the inherent human drive for learning and growth remains a fundamental motivator throughout the educational voyage.

Artificial Intelligence (AI) and Technology in Education Delivery.

Artificial Intelligence (AI) is set to significantly influence the future of formal school education, challenging the foundations of school funding and governance agendas. AI-powered adaptive learning platforms create personalised learning experiences tailored to each student's needs by continuously assessing performance and adjusting the curriculum in real-time to address learning gaps and provide individualised education (Holmes, Bialik, & Fadel, 2019). Intelligent Tutoring Systems (ITS) further personalise instruction by interpreting student responses and offering customised feedback, ensuring targeted support for each learner (VanLehn, 2011). Additionally, AI-driven learning analytics collect and analyse vast amounts of data from various educational activities, helping educators identify patterns and trends in student performance and make informed decisions on how to support individual learners effectively (Daniel, 2015).

AI also enhances teaching tools by providing sophisticated resources that streamline administrative tasks and improve educational outcomes. Automated grading systems reduce the workload on teachers, allowing them to focus more on instructional activities (Jordan & Mitchell, 2009). AI assists in creating smart content, such as interactive textbooks and digital courses, that adapt to student progress and enhance understanding (Nkuyubwatsi, 2016). Furthermore, AI-powered virtual assistants manage classroom logistics, answer routine student questions, and provide reminders about deadlines and events, freeing teachers to engage more deeply with their students (Wambalaba & Datta, 2018). AI-powered tools offer detailed insights into student performance and engagement, enabling teachers to identify struggling students, adjust teaching strategies, and provide targeted interventions (Bienkowski, Feng, & Means, 2012). AI also supports teacher professional development by recommending personalised training programs based on classroom data and teaching practices, ensuring that teachers continuously improve their skills and stay updated with the latest educational methodologies (Darling-Hammond, Hyler, & Gardner, 2017). These advancements promise to create a more efficient, equitable, and effective educational environment.

The relationship between school funding governance agendas and the rising AI education revolution is multifaceted and significant. As AI increasingly influences education, the allocation of school funding must adapt to support these technological advancements effectively. This requires substantial investment in technology infrastructure, including hardware, software, and educator training. School funding governance agendas must prioritise these investments to ensure schools are equipped with AI tools and resources. Additionally, policies must be implemented to guarantee equitable distribution of AI resources, ensuring all students have access regardless of socio-economic background. One of the primary concerns with the rise of AI in education is the potential for increased inequality. School funding governance must ensure that AI tools and resources are equitably distributed across all schools, including underfunded and rural areas, to bridge the digital divide.

Moreover, AI has the potential to transform curricula by providing personalised learning experiences and real-time feedback. School funding governance must support the development and integration of AI-driven curricula, including funding for research, pilot programs, and ongoing evaluation of AI-integrated curricula. The use of AI in education raises significant concerns regarding data privacy and ethics. School funding governance must address these issues by implementing policies and safeguards that protect student data and ensure ethical AI use. This involves funding for robust data privacy regulations and training for educators and administrators on ethical AI use. Additionally, adequate training and ongoing support for teachers and administrators are crucial for effective AI integration. By prioritising investments in technology infrastructure, curriculum development, and professional development, and addressing equity and data privacy, school funding governance can support the successful integration of AI in education, enhancing educational outcomes and ensuring all students benefit from AI advancements.

Technology Driven Teaching and Learning Modes

Homeschooling, distance learning, and learning webs represent alternative educational models that cater to diverse learning needs and preferences. Homeschooling allows parents to tailor their children's education to individual strengths and interests, often resulting in a highly personalised learning experience. This approach provides flexibility in curriculum design, pacing, and the integration of practical life skills. Distance learning, on the other hand, leverages digital technologies to deliver education remotely, enabling students to access high-quality instruction regardless of geographical constraints. Learning webs, a concept popularised by Ivan Illich (1971), envision a decentralised network of educational resources and opportunities, promoting self-directed learning and community engagement. These models collectively challenge the traditional classroom setup and offer promising avenues for a more adaptable and inclusive educational landscape.

The integration of Artificial Intelligence (AI) in these educational models can significantly enhance their effectiveness and reach. In homeschooling, AI can provide personalised learning plans and real-time feedback, helping parents identify areas where their children need additional support or enrichment. AI-powered educational tools and resources can offer interactive lessons, virtual tutors, and adaptive assessments, making homeschooling more comprehensive and engaging (Holmes, Bialik, & Fadel, 2019). For distance learning, AI can streamline administrative tasks, facilitate online collaboration, and provide predictive analytics to improve student outcomes. Intelligent Tutoring Systems (ITS) can offer personalised assistance to students, while AI-driven learning analytics can help educators track progress and adjust instructional strategies accordingly (VanLehn, 2011).

Looking towards the future, AI has the potential to revolutionise learning webs by connecting learners to a vast array of resources, mentors, and peer networks. AI can curate educational content based on individual learning preferences and goals, ensuring that learners have access to the most relevant and effective materials. Additionally, AI can facilitate the creation of virtual learning communities, where students can collaborate, share knowledge, and receive mentorship from experts worldwide. This global connectivity can democratise education, breaking down barriers to access and fostering a culture of lifelong learning. As AI continues to advance, it will play a crucial role in shaping the future of homeschooling, distance learning, and learning webs, making education more personalised, flexible, and inclusive.

Hidden Driver of Economic Prosperity Reflected in the Human Development Index

Despite a gloomy outlook in educational achievement based on popular indicators like test scores and per capita funding distribution, Australia performs relatively well on international socio-economic indicators. It is crucial to examine Australia's macro-level performance in socio-economic terms compared to the international community. These indicators reflect the country's inherent socio-economic prosperity, driven by continuous economic growth and social advancement.

Australia consistently secures a place in the very high human development category as per the United Nations Development Programme (UNDP), which annually publishes the Human Development Index (HDI). HDI is a composite measure of life expectancy, education, and per capita income, classifying countries into four tiers (very high, high, medium, and low) of human development.

In terms of HDI, Australia consistently ranks among the top tier of countries globally (10th in 2023). Only Switzerland, Norway, Iceland, Hong Kong, Denmark, Sweden, Germany, Ireland, and Singapore surpass Australia in 2023.

Australia typically boasts a high life expectancy, reflecting its advanced healthcare system and overall quality of life. Longer life expectancy contributes positively to Australia's HDI score. Life expectancy at birth in Australia stands at around 83.2 years, two years higher than the OECD average of 81 years. For women, life expectancy is 85 years, compared to 81 for men (OECD Better Life Index 2023), with Japan, Switzerland, Korea, and Spain ranking higher.

However, a notable discrepancy exists in life expectancies between indigenous and non-indigenous populations, with males at 71.6 and females at 75.6 in 2017 (Australian Institute of Health and Welfare).

Australia places significant emphasis on education, reflected in its populace's high levels of educational attainment. Access to quality education, spanning primary, secondary, and tertiary levels, contributes to Australia's robust performance in the HDI.

In 2022, Australia scored 21.1 in expected years of schooling (HDI value capped at 18 years). High expected years of schooling are typically associated with developed countries boasting well-established education systems, strong government investment in education, and cultural values prioritising learning and skill development. This indicator reflects a country's educational opportunities, quality of education provided, personal fulfillment, economic productivity, and effectiveness of educational policies and programs.

Moreover, Australia surpasses the OECD average in adult upper secondary education completion, with 84% of adults aged 25-64 having attained this level. The average student in Australia also outperforms the OECD average in reading literacy, mathematics, and science, scoring 499 compared to the OECD average of 488.

Gender disparities in education and income are considered in the HDI. Australia generally performs well in gender equality metrics, with relatively high levels of female participation in education and the workforce.

While Australia has made strides in reducing the gender wage gap, it persists, with women earning around 85-90% of men's wages for comparable work. Women remain underrepresented in senior leadership positions across various sectors, although they have achieved gender parity in education and have access to comprehensive healthcare services.

Australia's performance in the Human Development Index reflects its status as a developed nation with economic prosperity, a high standard of living, robust healthcare and education systems, and a relatively equitable society. However, ongoing efforts are necessary to address issues such as indigenous disadvantage, income inequality, and environmental sustainability.

The debate is all about doing better and closing the gaps at the micro level. We stress that there are many factors we should take into consideration.

Chapter 25

The Pursuit of Equity: Emerging Comparative Perspectives & Concluding Comments

Recapitulating the Journey

This publication has taken a comprehensive journey through the intricate landscape of school funding and governance in Australia, with a specific focus on Victoria. As we conclude, it is essential to recap, revisit the key themes, empirical findings, and insights that have emerged from our exploration. Connecting the empirical evidence gathered for this publication with broader research on funding distribution methods, school choice, autonomy, and governance is crucial.

The Dual Schooling System

Australia has a dual schooling system consisting of both government and non-government schools funded by federal and state governments, which is central to the nation's educational framework. The development of this structure is deeply connected to Australia's unique historical context, tracing back to the first settlement of New South Wales. Compared to other OECD countries, Australia has a notably high prevalence of non-government schools. Neoliberal policies promoting school choice and competition have significantly influenced this system, reinforcing the dual structure where both sectors receive state funding. Notably, the non-government school sector in Australia is steadily growing, presenting challenges to the pursuit of equity.

Federal and State Roles in School Funding

Since the 1990s, the Commonwealth Government has played a pivotal role in school funding by establishing agreements with state governments. The introduction of the Gonski review in 2011 marked a critical shift towards equity-based funding, emphasising the need for resources to be allocated based on need rather than the type of school. The Australian Education Act 2013 further solidified this approach through the Schooling Resource Standard funding allocation method. Despite mixed results, school funding has gained significant attention over the years, providing ample opportunities to drive the country's agenda for equity.

Innovations in Victoria's School Funding

Victoria has been at the forefront of innovative school governance and funding reforms since the 1990s. The state's shift towards operational autonomy for schools has enhanced school choice and competition. The School Resource Package (SRP), a formula-based funding system, has been instrumental in ensuring equity in resource allocation. School councils, established as legal entities, play a critical role in managing funds and strategic planning, balancing local needs with broader educational goals. Despite the complexities presented by the neoliberal economic model popular at the time, Victoria made a reasonable effort in experimenting with and trialling reforms to achieve equity, becoming a prominent state in this regard.

Effectiveness of the Methods of School Funding Distribution

This publication (chapters 10, 11, and 12) outlines the funding distribution methods and formulas designed to address horizontal and vertical equity in education. The considerations used in developing these formulas were comprehensive and paradigm-shifting. However, these formulas involve complex multiple components, adjustments, and weightings based on various factors such as student needs, school location, and specific programs. This complexity can make it challenging for those without a background in education finance to fully grasp how funds are allocated and how results can be assessed.

While formula-based school funding is inherently intricate, it is possible for parents and the public to understand it through clear, transparent, and accessible information. Effective communication is crucial in addressing concerns about fairness, equity, and the impact of funding on educational outcomes. By demystifying the allocation process, stakeholders can better appreciate the efforts made to ensure equitable resource distribution across schools.

Victoria's system of formula-based funding for public schools aims to allocate resources equitably based on individual student needs and equity considerations. This model incorporates both conventional and innovative equity measures to ensure fair distribution of state funds. The system is designed to support autonomous school governance, allowing schools to utilise funds effectively at the local level. Specific vertical equity funding initiatives target at-risk students to help them achieve literacy and numeracy goals and complete their education.

There are some suggestions for improving the foundations used to develop methods of funding distribution. For example, Glen Fahey (Fahey, 2020) argues that the current approach assumes that historical funding received by high-achieving schools represents the efficient cost of delivering quality education, which seems to be inaccurate. Base resourcing can be allocated according to the benchmark of the most efficient schools, not historical spending. Another suggestion by Fahey is that funding should be more outcomes-based and less inputs-based, including performance-based funding approaches for schools and teachers. The current model, based on student numbers and demographics, seems to offer few incentives to improve education quality.

Despite various efforts, the effectiveness of Victoria's funding system in reducing inequality remains contentious. Compensatory mechanisms like needs-based funding partially address these inequities but fall short due to a lack of transparency and fair redistribution. The generous public funding for non-government sectors and the uneven capacity of schools to raise additional resources contribute to structural maldistribution. Federal policies maintain this imbalance, as seen with the Gonski reforms, which ensure that well-resourced private schools do not lose funding. This complex interplay of public and private interests raises questions about the true nature of public education and its role in promoting equity.

Performance data shows a persistent achievement gap between Indigenous and non-Indigenous students in provincial areas, highlighting the need for more targeted funding. The impact of equity funding on narrowing the performance gap for students who do not speak English as their first language remains unclear. Additionally, socio-economic factors, such as parents' education and occupation, continue to significantly influence student outcomes. These disparities undermine the system's ability to address inequality effectively, suggesting that a more nuanced approach is necessary to ensure equitable distribution of resources and support for all students.

Effectiveness of School Governance

School Autonomy – Choice and Competition

This publication provides an in-depth account of the Victorian school governance model and its intricate mechanisms, which is typically not accessible to external researchers unless through longitudinal or ethnographic research. This section briefly recaptures these aspects.

While the Victorian model of devolved governance was expected to yield significant benefits, it also presents notable challenges. The devolved governance model possesses intrinsic strengths, such as the capacity to address local educational needs and enhance community engagement. However, this model also promotes unexpected vulnerabilities.

Managing Victorian schools involves addressing financial and operational risks inherent to the devolution model. This publication highlights several governance risks, such as budget deficits, mismatched strategic goals and local resources, losses from trading operations, ineffective systems, and unaccountable financial practices. Additionally, the study exposes the volatility of systems that allow for prevalent financial irregularities. These challenges reflect the complexities of aligning school-level autonomy with overarching strategic objectives and fiscal responsibilities.

The empirical research in this publication identifies specific governance challenges faced by individual schools, principals, teachers, and school councils. Schools have become isolated from one another, losing opportunities for collaboration and becoming burdened by increasing administrative tasks. Autonomy has brought diverse local actors into decision-making, creating uneasy partnerships in governance. The demand for good governance to address local needs has increased, but this is impacted by the expanded managerial roles and the requirements for marketing and promoting schools in an invisible competition. School autonomy has altered the professional identity of principals, who now focus on routines and exhibit vulnerable leadership styles. School councils face challenges in balancing educational interests with financial management responsibilities, often constrained by local capacity limitations.

Neoliberal economic and education policies have significantly impacted teachers by emphasising accountability and performance metrics, often based on student test scores, leading to increased stress and a narrowed curriculum focused on test preparation. These policies have intensified teachers' workloads with added administrative tasks and reporting requirements, contributing to longer working hours, burnout, and job dissatisfaction. Furthermore, the marketisation and privatisation trends introduce job insecurity and shift the focus from educational quality to profit-making, exacerbating inequities and altering teachers' roles.

Devolution has introduced corporate values and general management principles into loosely coupled educational institutions where human and social interaction is paramount. It has also led to increased centralisation or bureaucratisation, with growing influence from central and regional actors. This situation has created a devolution paradox where compliance-centred educational leadership is evolving, deviating from the core focus on learning and teaching processes. Consequently, the intended benefits of school autonomy are undermined by the practical challenges and systemic issues identified in the Victorian model.

Other Perspectives on Choice and Competition

Research in the Anglo-Saxon world has long examined the effects of school choice, highlighting both its advocates and critics. Proponents argue that parental choice is a human right that can improve educational opportunities, especially for disadvantaged students. Critics, however, believe that market mechanisms in education undermine public schooling values and exacerbate social inequalities. The OECD has noted the global spread of school choice policies since 1994, including voucher systems and the removal of public school catchment areas. Despite the complementary growth of school choice and private schooling, more research is needed to understand their interrelation and broader impacts on educational equity.

Market-oriented reforms have significantly impacted public education, particularly regarding equity and accountability. The intersection of equity agendas with market logics has introduced complexities and contradictions, focusing on performance measurement, comparison, and accountability as drivers of educational improvement. Marketisation appears to influence the conceptualisation and enactment of equity, highlighting tensions between efficiency, competition, and social justice goals. It is crucial to critically analyse the implications of market-driven policies on governance, human capital perspectives, and the broader social and economic rationales shaping education policy and practice (Savage, et. al, 2013, Savage, G. C, 2019).

Several key arguments challenge the notion that school autonomy improves student outcomes. Cobbold (2014) suggests that various studies and reports reveal that the impact of school autonomy on student achievement is either trivial or negative, contradicting the assertions made by proponents of this approach. The Productivity Commission (2012) has noted that the effects of delegating decision-making to schools are mixed. While some studies indicate potential benefits, others show that greater autonomy could exacerbate inequalities, particularly affecting disadvantaged students.

Australia has a higher concentration of disadvantaged students in disadvantaged schools compared to similar OECD countries. Nationally, government schools enrol 59.3 percent of secondary school students but disproportionately serve the largest share of students with disabilities (76.4 percent), Indigenous students (79.4 percent), and the lowest mathematics achievers (76.2 percent). This results in a highly uneven distribution of disadvantaged secondary school-aged Australians across different school sectors.

International evidence further complicates the debate. Studies from countries such as New Zealand and the United States reveal that increased school autonomy has not led to significant gains in student achievement. For instance, charter schools in the US have not consistently outperformed traditional public schools, challenging the belief that autonomy is a key factor in improving educational outcomes. The Centre for Research on Education Outcomes (CREDO) at Stanford University found in a 2009 study that only 17% of charter schools performed better than traditional public schools, while 37% performed worse, and 46% showed no significant difference (CREDO, 2009).

Additionally, the findings on school autonomy's effects are contradictory. While some studies of academies in England report improvements, others show no impact on student achievement (Academies Commission, 2013). This inconsistency underscores the need for a more comprehensive approach to education reform. Critics suggest that high-quality systems of teacher development, appraisal, and feedback may be more crucial for improving student outcomes than focusing solely on autonomy.

The Grattan Institute's report (Jensen, 2013) highlights the limitations of relying solely on school competition and autonomy to improve educational outcomes. While efforts to increase competition among schools have had marginal impacts, the significant structural issues and market failures in education hinder systemic improvement. Transparency initiatives like the My School website have not led to substantial performance gains. Similarly, the effectiveness of school autonomy is questioned due to poor strategy and implementation, with both highly autonomous and centralised schools often continuing ineffective practices.

Managerialism

School autonomy can theoretically bring fresh perspectives and innovative approaches to school administration. However, autonomy may also introduce managerial and corporate values that prioritise bureaucratic processes, potentially undermining educational outcomes. In some cases, increased autonomy may result in a focus on administrative tasks rather than educational leadership, leading to a disconnection between managerial decisions and the needs of students and teachers.

The trend towards school choice and autonomy infuses new management principles into educational administration, based on private sector values of efficiency and productivity. These principles are designed to regulate educational bodies with an emphasis on output over process. This shift endorses strong market-type accountability in spending within the educational sector, where achieving financial and other targets becomes a priority. Consequently, this transformation changes the ethical governance framework from public welfare principles to commercial norms of value-for-money. Lynch (2014) notes that this shift moves away from the traditional focus on citizen rights, welfare, and solidarity, towards treating students as customers and service users, with an emphasis on competition and performance indicators.

Managerialism presents specific challenges to principals, teachers, and students. While managing a school requires various technical skills such as planning, budgeting, and time management, the unique developmental and nurturing aspects of education are often undervalued by corporate culture. Educational leaders need to support teachers in fostering student growth and development, which requires an emotional investment not typically seen in the private sector. This managerial approach, originating from commercial contexts, risks subordinating the educational process to output and profit metrics. Lynch, Grummell, and Devine (2012) argue that such an approach could undermine the relational and developmental principles central to teaching and learning, leading to a polarised focus between student welfare and efficiency gains. Consequently, while the educational management environment is evolving, there is a risk that committed school leaders may be overlooked in terms of recognition, advancement, and reward, as managerialism may present more weaknesses than strengths when applied to educational administration.

Social Justice

This book presents evidence suggesting that non-government schools ultimately benefit more from federal and state funding distribution methods. The analysis indicates that these funding mechanisms disproportionately favour non-government schools, resulting in a higher allocation of resources compared to public institutions.

Angus (2015) critically examines how neoliberal education policies, particularly school choice, emphasise market principles like competition, efficiency, and individualism. These policies shape educational landscapes by affecting accessibility and quality, often exacerbating educational inequalities. Angus argues that school choice policies disproportionately benefit affluent families, giving them greater access to preferred schools and creating a more stratified education system. He highlights how these policies prioritise consumerist values over educational equity, leading to significant socio-economic divides. The rhetoric of choice and freedom, often used to justify these policies, obscures the resulting inequalities.

In neoliberal education policies, education is commodified, and individual success is regarded as paramount. Angus advocates for a more inclusive approach that addresses structural inequalities and considers the collective good. Neoliberal education policies impact equity and social justice, necessitating a re-evaluation of policies that prioritise market mechanisms over democratic educational values. The privatisation of schools under neoliberal policies has intensified inequalities between advantaged and disadvantaged groups, maintaining social segregation and privileges for affluent families.

Private schooling, managed to guarantee advantages, perpetuates these disparities by protecting affluent children from potential social risks posed by diverse environments. Thus, families often choose private schools to maintain their privileged positions and keep their children away from perceived dangers associated with other social groups.

The entanglement of public and private interests, particularly through generous funding for private schools and the increasing involvement of the private sector in public education governance, compromises redistributive justice (Keddie et al., 2020). This trend has led to greater systemic inequities and undermines the notion of education as a common good. To uphold public education ideals, there is a need for a nuanced understanding of public interest and accountability, especially concerning private sector roles. The ongoing conceptualisation of public education for the common good requires critically engaging with the paradoxes of economic efficiency, competition, and individualism inherent in school autonomy reform.

School autonomy reform in Australia aims to enhance school and system performance by granting schools greater decision-making freedom over finance, resourcing, and staffing. However, other research challenges this thesis by highlighting the negative social justice implications of market-driven autonomy. Discourses of devolution, economic efficiency, competition, and individualism have weakened structural support for public schools, exacerbated stratification, and disadvantaged rural, low SES, and small schools. These practices undermine the collective approach to education as a public good, raising concerns about the equity and inclusiveness of school autonomy (Keddie et al., 2020).

Keddie (2017) suggests that school autonomy reform can enhance social justice by granting principals more management flexibility and parents greater school choice. This can lead to political justice by giving stakeholders a voice in governance, cultural justice by recognising marginalised cultures, and economic justice by distributing resources more equitably. However, if not carefully managed, school autonomy can also undermine social justice by exacerbating existing inequalities due to resource maldistribution and accountability pressures.

In Australia, centralised authority and redistributive policies such as the Gonski reforms are crucial for ensuring that school autonomy supports social justice. These mechanisms can align representative and recognitive politics with redistributive efforts to improve participation equity within schools. A socially just approach to autonomy will focus on overcoming domination and oppression, supporting democratic professional autonomy, recognising marginalised groups, and directing resources to disadvantaged students (Keddie, 2017).

Legal Fairness

The legality of the school funding system in Australia, particularly regarding the funding of non-government schools, has evolved through historical context, court rulings, and changes in government policy (Patty, 2019). The debate over whether non-government schools should receive public funding began with a notable incident in 1962 involving St Brigid's Catholic School in Goulburn. Over the years, Catholic and independent school lobby groups have successfully secured a significant share of government funding.

The distribution of school funding in Australia has been contentious, with data from various sources (Goss, 2017; Cobbold, 2024) and in this publication (Chapter 23) showing that, while government schools receive most of the state and federal funding, Catholic and independent schools receive a higher proportion of their funding targets. This disparity has raised concerns about the equity of funding distribution, as public schools often operate below their funding needs. Changes in the interpretation of the Australian Constitution have also questioned the legality of special deals favouring certain religious schools. Section 116 of the Constitution prohibits laws establishing religion, which has implications for how funds are allocated to religious schools.

Legal experts argue that if government funding of religious schools is discriminatory, it could be constitutionally invalid. The landmark High Court decision in the 1981 DOGS case affirmed public funding for non-government schools, based on the understanding that the funding was non-discriminatory. Recent debates have focused on whether funding formulas have favoured Catholic schools, particularly those serving high socio-economic status families. Critics argue that such funding practices could violate the constitutional prohibition against preferential treatment. The government's promise to end "special deals" and ensure fair, needs-based funding aligns with constitutional requirements and international obligations to provide equitable education for all children.

Constitutional law scholars, including George Williams and Luke Beck (2020), note that the High Court is generally reluctant to overturn its previous rulings (Lee, 2020). They argue that the DOGS case has led the federal government to believe it can fund religious groups without constitutional restrictions, leaving only political limits. However, they suggest that legal challenges to certain aspects of public funding for religious schools could still succeed despite the DOGS decision. Specifically, they doubt the constitutionality of favouring specific religions with federal educational funds or providing money for explicitly religious purposes, like building chapels or mosques. If these issues arise in the future, the High Court will need to re-examine the DOGS case decision (Patty, 2019).

Problem at Hand

Overall, social segregation in Australian schooling, intensified by a neoliberal emphasis on choice and privatisation, remains a pressing concern. Over the past four decades, the social divide between private and public schools has widened, with private institutions enrolling more students from affluent families. Australia shows a strong correlation between socio-economic background and academic achievement.

Efforts to address funding disparities, such as the Gonski Review, face obstacles due to vested interests and political debates. The main political parties' commitment to consumer choice as a means of achieving educational excellence and parity poses significant social and political challenges. Nevertheless, both federal and state governments continue to strive for greater equity in education through policy measures, funding initiatives, and support programs, emphasising the necessity of ongoing targeted interventions to achieve sustained progress towards educational equity nationwide.

Prospects

Australia is enjoying sustained socio-economic prosperity and high social democracy. At a post-neoliberal crossroads, the nation addresses challenges like reducing educational disparities and socio-economic inequalities while ensuring universal access to quality education. The shift towards holistic education, including global citizenship education, prepares students for an interconnected world. Key challenges include reinvesting in public education to foster social cohesion and economic prosperity. Despite these challenges, the prospects for constructive transformation remain healthy, with innovative and ongoing efforts particularly notable in Victoria. This book contributes to the debate on future directions, emphasising the importance of continued efforts to achieve educational equity and inclusivity.

Appendix 1

Bibliography

Academies Commission. (2013). Unleashing Greatness: Getting the Best from an Academised System. RSA.

Angrist, J., & Lang, K. (2004). Does School Integration Generate Peer Effects? Evidence from Boston's Metco Program. American Economic Review, 94 (5), 1613-1634.

Angus, L. (2015). School Choice: Neoliberal Education Policy and Imagined Futures. British Journal of Sociology of Education 36(3):1-19. DOI:10.1080/01425692.2013.823835.

Apple, M. W. (2004). Ideology and Curriculum. Routledge.

Ashenden, D. (2016) Money, school and politics: Some FAQs. Inside Story. http://insidestory.org.au/money-schools-and-politics-some-faqs. Accessed 12 Oct 2016.

Austin, A. G. (1963). Australian Education, 1788-1900: Church, State and Public Education in Colonial Australia. Pitman.

Australian Bureau of Statistics (ABS). https://www.abs.gov.au/statistics.

Australian Council for Educational Research (ACER). (2019). Australian education review. ACER Press.

Australian Council for Educational Research (ACER). (2019). Language backgrounds and achievement in NAPLAN: A report for the NSW Department of Education. https://www.acer.org.

Australian Council for the Defence of Government Schools (DOGS). https://www.adogs.info/ .

Australian Curriculum, Assessment and Reporting Authority (ACARA). https://acara.edu.au/reporting.

Australian Curriculum, Assessment and Reporting Authority. ACARA. (2022). NAPLAN National Report. Australian Curriculum, Assessment and Reporting Authority.

Australian Curriculum, Assessment and Reporting Authority. ACARA. My School Data.

Australian Department of Education. https://www.education.gov.au/schooling.

Australian Education Union. (2012). Devolution and Education. A Research Report.

Australian Education Union. https://www.aeufederal.org.au

Australian Government. (2023). Improving Outcomes for All Australian Government Summary Report of the Review to Inform a Better and Fairer Education System, 2023.

Australian Government. (2024). Review of the National Agreement on Closing the Gap Study report Volume 1 January 2024.

Australian Government. (2023). Australian Education Regulations 2023 made under the Australian Education Act 2013.

Australian Institute of Health and Welfare. (2017). Life expectancy and mortality of Aboriginal and Torres Strait Islander people.

Australian National Audit Office. (2003). Public Sector Governance, Volume 1, Better Practice Guide. Commonwealth of Australia, Canberra. ACT.

Ball, S. J. (2003). The teacher's soul and the terrors of performativity. Journal of Education Policy, 18(2), 215-228.

Ball, S. J. (2012). Global Education Inc.: New Policy Networks and the Neo-Liberal Imaginary. Routledge.

Bandaranayake, B. (2011). Fraud Prevention. Inspire Magazine. December 2011 Issue. The Department of Education and Training, Melbourne. Victoria, Australia.

Bandaranayake, B. (2013). Formula-Based School Funding System in Victoria: An Empirical Analysis of Equity. NCPEA International Journal of Educational Leadership Preparation, Vol. 8, No. 2. pp 191-207.

Bandaranayake, B. (2014) Fraud and corruption control at education system level: A case study of the Victorian Department of Education and Training. Journal of Cases in Education Leadership. Vol 17:4 PP 34-53. Sage publications.

Bandaranayake, B. (2015). Taking the Mystery Out of School Financing in Victoria, Australia: A Devolve Financial Management and Governance Model. November 2015. National Council of Professors of Educational Administration.

Bandaranayake, B. (2016). Polarisation of high-performing and low-performing secondary schools in Victoria, Australia: an analysis of causal complexities. The Australian Educational Researcher. Aug 201643(5). DOI:10.1007/s13384-016-0213-8.

Baxendale, R (2014). Anti-autonomy stance "shows Andrew in thrall of union". The Australian, 15 December 2014.

Behrendt, L. (2019). Indigenous Australia for Dummies. Wiley Publishing.

Belley, P., Frenette, M., & Lochner. L. (2011). Post-secondary Attendance by Parental Income in the U.S. and Canada: What Role for Financial Aid Policy? EPRI Working Paper No. 2011-3. Ontario: Economic Policy Research Institute.

BenDavid-Hadar, Iris. (2018). Education Finance, Equality, and Equity. Editor. 2018. Springer.

Bentley, T; Savage, Glenn C. (2017). Educating Australia: Challenges for the decade ahead. Melbourne University.

Berne, R., & Stiefel, L. (1984). The Measurement of Equity in School Finance: Conceptual, Methodological, and Empirical Dimensions. Johns Hopkins University Press.

Berne, R., & Stiefel, L. (1999). Concepts of School Finance Equity: 1970 to the Present. In H. F. Ladd, R. Chalk, & J. S. Hansen (Eds.), Equity and Adequacy in Education Finance: Issues and Perspectives (pp. 7-33). National Academy Press.

Bienkowski, M., Feng, M., & Means, B. (2012). Enhancing teaching and learning through educational data mining and learning analytics: An issue brief. U.S. Department of Education.

Blinder, A. S. (1988). Keynesian Economics: The View from John Maynard Keynes. New York: Palgrave Macmillan.

Bourdieu, P. (1973). Cultural Reproduction and Social Reproduction. In R. Brown (Ed), Knowledge, Education, and Cultural Change. (pp. 71-112). London: Tavistock Publications.

Bourdieu, P., & Passeron J. C. (1977). Reproduction in Education, Society and Culture. Beverly Hills, CA: Sage.

Brenner, N. (2004). New State Spaces: Urban Governance and the Rescaling of Statehood. Oxford University Press.

Buckingham, J. (2010). The rise of religious Schools. The Centre for Independent Studies. Australia.

Burke, G. and Spaull, A. (2001). Education and Training. Centenary Article - Australian schools: participation and funding 1901-2000 (Year Book Australia, 2001), last modified 18 Sep 2001, http://www.abs.gov.au.

Cahill, R., and Gray, J. (2010). Funding and Secondary Schools Choice in Australia: A Historical Consideration. Australian Journal of Teacher Education. Vol. 35, 1. February 2010.

Caldwell, B. J. (2002). Autonomy and Self-management: Concepts and Evidence. In T. Bush, and L. Bell, L (Ed.), The Principles and Practice of Educational Management (pp. 24 – 40. London: Paul Chapman Publishing.

Caldwell, B. J. and Spinks, J. M (1988). The Self-Managing School, Routledge.

Campbell, C., and Proctor, H (2014). A History of Australian Schooling. Allen and Unwin. Australia.

Canvan, K. (2012). Federalism, Whitlam and the Funding for Catholic schools in a peculiarly historical context. Whitlam Institute. University of Western Sydney. Australia.

Carnoy, M., & Levin, H. M. (1985). Schooling and Work in the Democratic State. Stanford, CA: Stanford University Press.

Caves. K; Bandaranayake. B; Schenker-Wicki, A. (2015). Is Formula-Based Equity Funding Enough: A Configurational Analysis of School Achievements in Victoria, Australia. Conference paper. American Educational Research Association.

Centre for the Study of Higher Education. (2008). Participation and Equity: A Review of the Participation in Higher Education of People from Low Socioeconomic Backgrounds and Indigenous People. Melbourne: University of Melbourne

Chapman, D. (2002). Corruption and the Education Sector. Management Systems International. 600 Water Street. SW. Washington. DC. 20024 USA.

Chubb, J. E., & Moe, T. M. (1990). Politics, Markets, and America's Schools. Brookings Institution Press.

Coalition's Policy for Schools: Students First. (2013). http://www.liberal.org.au/latest-news/2013/08/29/

Cobbold, T. (2020). New Figures Show Huge Funding Increases for Private Schools & Cuts to Public Schools. Education Research Paper. Save Our Schools.

Cobbold, T. (2014). Pyne's School Autonomy Myth. Choice and competition Winter 2014 issue of Dissent Magazine.

Cobbold, T. (2014). School Autonomy: Does it Improve Student Outcomes? Save Our Schools. http://saveourschools.com.au/

Cobbold, T. (2020). Government funding in Australian schools. Save Our Schools.

Cobbold, T. (2024, March 24). Analysis of funding disparities in Australian schools. Save Our Schools.

Coleman, J. S. (1966). Equality of Educational Opportunity. U.S. Department of Health, Education, and Welfare, Office of Education.

Collier, P., & Venables, A. J. (2008). Trade and Economic Performance: Does Africa's Fragmentation Matter?. World Bank.

Commonwealth of Australia Constitution Act 1901. (The Constitution).

Commonwealth of Australia. (2013). National Plan for School Improvement: Stronger. Smarter. Fairer. May 2013. http://www.budget.gov.au/2013.

Commonwealth of Australia. (2014). Towards Responsible Government. The Report of the National Commission of Audit. Phase One. February 2014.

Commonwealth of Australia. (2018). Closing the Gap: Prime Minister's Report 2018. Australian Government.

Connell, R. (2012). Ideology of the marketplace underpins school reforms. The Drum, ABC. http://www.abc.net.au/news/2012-03-16/connell-ideology-of-the-marketplace-underpins-school-22reforms/3892492.

Connell, R. (2013). The neoliberal cascade and education: An essay on the market agenda and its consequences. Critical Studies in Education, 54(2), 99-112.

Connell, R. et al. (1982). Making the difference: schools, families and social division. George Allen and Unwin, Sydney.

Conran, Peter. (2020). Review of COAG Councils and Ministerial Forums Report to National Cabinet, October 2020. Department of Prime Minister & Cabinet.

Courpasson, D. (2000). Managerial strategies in domination: Power in soft bureaucracies. Organisation Studies. 21 (1), Pages 141-161.

CREDO, (2009). Multiple Choice: Charter School Performance in 16 States. Centre for Research on Education Outcomes (CREDO), Stanford University http://credo.stanford.edu

Crouch, C. (2011). The Strange Non-death of Neoliberalism. Polity Press.

Daniel, B. K. (2015). Big Data and analytics in higher education: Opportunities and challenges. British Journal of Educational Technology, 46(5), 904-920.

Darling-Hammond, L., Hyler, M. E., & Gardner, M. (2017). Effective Teacher Professional Development. Learning Policy Institute.

Day, C., & Smethem, L. (2009). The effects of reform: Have teachers really lost their sense of professionalism? Journal of Educational Change, 10(2-3), 141-157.

Deming, David J., Justine S. Hastings, Thomas J. Kane, and Douglas O. Staiger (ed) (2014). School Choice, School Quality, and Postsecondary Attainment. American Economic Review 2014, 104(3): 991–1013.

Department of Education (2024). Chart of Accounts for Victorian Government Schools January 2024 | v5.0.

Department of Education (2024). Indicative Student Resource Package Guide.

Department of Education (2024). Schools Workforce Planning Guide. 2024.

Department of Education and Training (DET). (2005). Fraud and Corruption Control Framework. Melbourne. Australia.

Department of Education and Training (DET). (2006). Victorian government financial assistance for non-government schools. Melbourne. Australia.

Department of Education, Science and Training. (2006). A History of State Aid to Non-Government Schools in Australia.

Department of Education, Skills and Employment. (2021). School Funding Assurance Framework.

Department of Education. (2014). Independent Public Schools. https://www.education.gov.au/independent-public-schools.

Department of Education. (2024). Finance Manual — Financial Management for Schools Policy last updated 30 November 2021, DET.

Department of Premier and Cabinet. (2007). Federalist paper 2: The Future of Schooling in Australia – A Report by States and Territories. Melbourne.

Devine, L D. (2012). State Aid for Education in Australia: An Overview. Administration and Research Papers and Journal Articles. http://research.avondale.edu.au/admin_papers/1.

Diefenbach, T. (2009). New Public Management in public sector organisations: The dark sides of managereilistic enlightenment. Public Administration. 87 (4), pages 892-909.

Dowling, A. (2007). Australia's S892-909chool Funding System. Policy Analysis and Program Evaluation Unit.

Eacott, S. (2011). Preparing 'educational' leaders in managerialist times: An Australian story. Journal of Educational Administration and History, 43(1), 43-59.

Economou, N and Ghazarian, Zareh (ed) (2022). Australian politics for Dummies, John Wiley & Sons Australia, Ltd.

Edgerton, J. D., & Roberts, L. W. (2014). Cultural Capital or Habitus? Bourdieu and Beyond in the Explanation of Enduring

Educational Inequality. Theory and Research in Education, 12 (2), 193-220. doi:10.1177/1477878514530231.

Education Council, (2019). Alice Springs (Mparntwe) Education Declaration.

Edwards, Meredith. Et. Al. (2011). Public Sector Governance in Australia. ANU. 2011.

Ergas, Henry and Pincus, Jonathan. (2011). Reflections on Fiscal Equalisation in Australia. * State Funding Forum, Realm Hotel, Canberra, 12-13 September 2011.

Fahey, G. (2017). Dollars and Sense: Time for smart reform of Australian school funding, The centre for Independent Studies. Research paper 40. 2017.

Fahey, G. (2020). Improving School Funding: Evidence-Based Reform for Better Student Outcomes. Centre for Independent Studies.

Farkas, G. (2003). Cognitive skills and non-cognitive traits and behaviors in stratification processes. Annual Review of Sociology, 29, 541-562.

Fazekas, M. (2012). School Funding Formulas: Review of Main Characteristics and Impacts. OECD Education Working papers No. 74. http://dx.doi.org/10.1787/5k993xw27cd3-en.

Field, S., Kuczera, M., and Pont, B. (2007). No More Failures: Ten Steps to Equity in Education. OECD. ISBN 978-92-64-03259-0, € 24.

Finnie, R., & Mueller, R. (2008). The Effects of Family Income, Parental Education and Other Background Factors on Access to Post-Secondary Education in Canada: Evidence from the YITS, Toronto: Educational Policy Institute.

Forsey, M., Davies, S., & Walford, G. (2017). The Globalisation of School Choice? Symposium Books.

Forsey, Martin. Proctor, Helen and Meghan, Stacey (2017). A Most Poisonous Debate: Legitimising Support for Australian Private Schools. In Private Schools and School Choice in Compulsory Education. P 49-66.

Frederickson, George (1999). Ethics and the New Managerialism. Public Administration & Management. 4, 2, 1999 pp. 299-324.

Frenette, M. (2007). Why Are Youth from Lower-Income Families Less Likely to Attend University? Evidence from Academic Abilities, Parental Influences, and Financial Constraints. Ottawa: Statistics Canada.

Friedman, M. (1962). Capitalism and Freedom. University of Chicago Press.

Gewirtz, S., Ball, S. J., & Bowe, R. (1995). Markets, Choice and Equity in Education. Open University Press.

Gibbons, S., & Telhaj, S. (2012). Peer Effects: Evidence from Secondary School Transition in England. IZA Discussion Paper, No. 6455. Bonn: Institute for the Study of Labor.

Gonski, D., Boston, K., Greiner, K., Lawrence, C., Scales, B., and Tannock, P. (2011). Review of Funding for Schooling. Department of Education, Employment and Workplace Relations. Canberra. Australia.

Goss, Peter. (2017). School funding is a journey, not a destination. Grattan Institute. 06.09.2017.

Government of Australia. (2020). National Agreement on Closing the Gap. July 2020.

Green, Andy, John Preston and Jan Germen Janmaat. (2006). Education, Equality and Social Cohesion: A Comparative Analysis. Palgrave. 2006.

Grubb, Norton. Rebecca Allen. (2011). Rethinking school funding, resources, incentives, and outcomes. Journal of Educ Change (2011) 12:121–130.

Gunter, H. M. (2012). Leadership and the reform of education. Policy Press.

Hallak, J., Poisson, M. (Ed). (2007). Governance in Education: Transparency and Accountability. International Institute of Educational Planning: Paris.

Hanushek, E. (2006). Schools Resources. In Handbook of the Economic of Education, Volume 2. E Hanushek and F. Welsh (Ed). Elsevier B.V.

Hanushek, E. A, Markman, K. J., & Rivkin, S. G. (2003). Does Peer Ability Affect Student Achievement? Journal of Applied Econometrics, 18 (5), 527-544. doi:10.1002/jae.741.

Hanushek, E. A. (2013). Financing Schools. In J. Hattie and E. M. Anderman (Eds) An International Guide to Student Achievement, (pp.134-136), London: Routledge.

Hanushek, E. A., & Wössmann, L. (2006). Does Educational Tracking Affect Performance and Inequality? Differences-in-Differences Evidence across Countries. The Economic Journal, 116 (510), C63-C76. doi:10.1111/j.1468-0297.2006.01076.x.

Hanushek, E., Link, S., Woesmann, L. (2012a). Does School Autonomy Make Sense Everywhere? Panel Estimates from PISA. http://www.adb.org.

Hanushek, E., Link, S., Woesmann, L. (2012b). Allowing Local Schools to Make More Decisions May Work in Developed Countries but is Questionable in Developing Countries. Vox Research-Based Policy Analysis. http://www.voxeu.org.php.

Hargreaves, A. (2003). Teaching in the Knowledge Society: Education in the Age of Insecurity. Teachers College Press.

Harrington, M. (2013). Funding the National Plan for Education Improvement: An Explanation. Parliament Library. Department of Parliament Services.

Harrington, M. (2014). Australian Government Funding for Schools Explained: 2013 update. Parliament Library. Department of Parliament Services.

Harvey, D. (2005). A Brief History of Neoliberalism. Oxford University Press.

Hattie, J. (2009). Visible Learning: A Synthesis of Over 800 Meta-Analyses Relating to Achievement. Routledge.

Hawke, Bob, (1990) Australian Labor Party, Speech Delivered at Brisbane, Qld, March 8th, 1990. https://electionspeeches.moadoph.gov.au.

Haydon, Graham (ed). (2110). Educational Equality. Continuum International Publishing Group. 2010.

Hayward, D (1990). Liberal Party State Council Education Speech. Melbourne.

Hayward, D (1995). Improving Student Learning in Schools of the Future. Presentation to Extending the Real Reform. Denver, Colorado, 12-14 July.

Hayward, D (1998). Schools of the Future. B. Caldwell and D Hayward (eds). The Future of Schools – Lessons from the Reform of Education. London: Fsalmer Press, 39-80.

Hinz, B. (2010). Australian Federalism and School Funding: Exploring the nexus in Victoria's Devolution Reforms. Australian Political Science Association Annual Conference, Melbourne 26-29 September 2010.

Hoggett, P. (1996). New Modes of control in the public service. Public Administration. 74.1. Pages 9-32.

Holmes, W., Bialik, M., & Fadel, C. (2019). Artificial Intelligence in Education: Promises and Implications for Teaching and Learning. Center for Curriculum Redesign.

Hugo, G. (2014). The Economic Contribution of Humanitarian Settlers in Australia. International Migration Review, 48(3), 587-617.

Hursh, D. (2007). Assessing No Child Left Behind and the rise of neoliberal education policies. American Educational Research Journal, 44(3), 493-518.

Illich, I. (1971). Deschooling Society. Harper & Row.

Independent Broad-based Anticorruption Commission (2015). http://www.ibac.vic.gov.au.

Independent Review into Regional, Rural and Remote Education. (2017). Australian Government Response.

Iris BenDavid-Hadar, Stephoni Case & Rob Smith (2017). School funding formulae: designed to create a learning society?, Compare: A Journal of Comparative and International Education, DOI: 10.1080/03057925.2017.1323625.

Jaensch, D., & Teicher, J. (2016). Australian Politics: Theory and Practice. Pearson.

Jensen, B. (2013). Catching Up: Learning from the Best School Systems in East Asia. Grattan Institute.

Jensen, B. 2013. The myth of markets in school education, Grattan Institute 2013.

Jeremy Moon, and Campbell Sharman (ed) (2003). Australian Politics and Government the Commonwealth, the State and the Territories.

Karmel, P. (1973). Schools in Australia: Report of the interim Committee for the Australian School Commission. Australian Government Publishing Service. Canberra.

Keating, J, Annett, P, Burke, G, and OHanlon, C. (2011). Mapping funding and regulatory arrangements across the Commonwealth and state and territories. The University of Melbourne. Melbourne. Australia.

Keating, J. (2009). A new federalism in Australian Education: A proposal for a national reform Agenda. Education Foundation.

Keating, J. (2011). Federalism in Real World. University of Melbourne.

Keddie, A, (2017). School autonomy reform and public education in Australia: implications for social justice. The Australian Educational Researcher · August 2017.

Keddie, A, et al. (2020), School autonomy, marketisation and social justice: The plight of principals and schools" the Journal of Educational Administration and History.

Keddie, A, et al. (2020), The constitution of school autonomy in Australian public education: Key areas of paradox for social justice". International Journal of Leadership in Education.

Keddie, A, et al. (2020). Mobilising School Autonomy for Social Justice: Narratives from Australia. Palgrave Macmillan.

Keddie, A, et al. (2020). The constitution of school autonomy in Australian public education: areas of paradox for social justice, International Journal of Leadership in Education, DOI: 10.1080/13603124.2020.1781934.

Keddie, A, et al. (2023). What needs to happen for school autonomy to be mobilised to create more equitable public schools and systems of education? The Australian Educational Researcher 50:1571–1597 https://doi.org/10.1007/s13384-022-00573-w.

Keddie, A. (2017). School Autonomy Reform and Social Justice: A Focus on the Power Relations of Neoliberalism. In G. T. L. Brown & L. Harris (Eds.), Handbook of Human and Social Conditions in Assessment (pp. 113-130). Routledge.

Kersten, T. A. (2014). Taking the Mystery out of Illinois School Finance. NCPEA Publications. National Council of Professors of Educational Administration. Michigan.

Keynes, J. M. (1936). The General Theory of Employment, Interest and Money. London: Macmillan and Company, Limited.

Koinzer, T, Nikolai, R and Waldow, Florian (2017), Private Schooling and School Choice as Global Phenomena: An Introduction. Springer.

Kraus, N. (2023). The Fantasy Economy Neoliberalism, Inequality, and the Education Reform Movement, Temple University Press, 2023.

Lamb, S., Jackson, J., Walstab, A., & Huo, S. (2015). Educational Opportunity in Australia 2015: Who Succeeds and Who Misses Out? Centre for International Research on Education Systems, Victoria University.

Lareau, A. (2002). Invisible Inequality: Social Class and Childrearing in Black Families and White Families. American Sociological Review, 67 (5), 747-776. doi:10.2307/3088916.

Lareau, A. (2011). Unequal Childhoods: Race, Class, and Family Life. Berkeley, CA: University of California.

Latham, M. (2001). Civilising Global Capital: New Thinking for Australian Labor. Allen & Unwin.

Lee, H. (2020). The Constitutionality of Public Funding for Religious Schools in Australia. Monash University Law Review, 46(1), 132-160.

Lee, Jane. (2020). The dog fight over school funding that went all the way to the High Court. ABC RN. Posted Tue 12 May 2020.

Levacic, R. (2008). Funding Schools by Formula: Comparing Practice in Five Countries. Journal of Education Finance, 33(3), 297-322.

Levacic, R., & Downes, P. (2004). Formula Funding of Schools, Decentralisation and Corruption: A Comparative Analysis. Comparative Education, 40(1), 93-109.

Lipman, P. (2011). The New Political Economy of Urban Education: Neoliberalism, Race, and the Right to the City. Routledge.

Lynch, K. (2014). New Managerialism: The impact on education. Concept. 5 (3). http://concept.lib.ed.ac.uk.

Lynch, K. (2014). New Managerialism in Education: Commercialisation, Carelessness and Gender. In B. Francis & C. Skelton (Eds.), The SAGE Handbook of Gender and Education (pp. 424-438). SAGE Publications.

Lynch, K. (2014). New Managerialism in Education: Commercialising Care. In New Managerialism in Education (pp. 1-12). Palgrave Macmillan, London.

Macdonald, Laura, and Ruckert, Arne. (2009). Post-Neoliberalism in the Americas. Palgrave Macmillan. 2009.

Maddern, I. T. (1969). A Short History of State Education in Victoria. The L V Printers. Traralgon. Australia.

Maddison, S., & Denniss, R. (2013). An Introduction to Australian Public Policy: Theory and Practice. Cambridge University Press.

McAllister, I. (2011). The Australian Voter: 50 Years of Change. UNSW Press.

McGrath, D. (1993). Equity in School Finance: Definitions and Comparisons. Journal of Education Finance, 18(3), 279-304.

McManus, Matthew (2020). The Rise of Post-Modern Conservatism Neoliberalism, Post-Modern Culture, and Reactionary Politics. Palgrave Macmillan.

Meier, V. (2004). Choosing between School Systems: The Risk of Failure. Finanzarchiv 60 (1), 83-93.

Miller, P. and Davey, I. (1990). Family formation, schooling and the patriarchal state. In: Theobald, M. R. and Selleck, R. J. W. (eds.) Family, school and state in Australian history. Sydney: Allen and Unwin.

Miller, P. W., & Voon, D. (2011). Lessons from My School. Australian Economic Review, 44 (4), 366-386. doi:10.1111/j.1467-8462.2011.00652.x.

Minister for Education (2024). Ministerial Order 1280. Constitution of Government School Councils. Version incorporating amendments as at 27 January 2024.

Mundine, Warren. (2024) From Measuring to merely Meeting. Productivity Commission misses mark on Closing the Gap. Policy Paper 57 | May 2024. The centre for Independent Studies.

Musset, P. (2012). School Choice and Equity: Current Policies in OECD Countries and a Literature Review. OECD Education Working Papers, No. 66, OECD Publishing.

National Commission of Audit. (2014). Towards Responsible Government: the report of the National Commission of Audit. http://www.ncoa.gov.au/report/phase-one/index.html

National School Resourcing Board. (2020). Review of needs-based funding requirements: Final report | December 2019. Australian Government.

Nkuyubwatsi, B. (2016). Leveraging informal digital learning to enhance formal education. E-Learning and Digital Media, 13(1-2), 1-4.

NSW Education Standards Authority (NESA). (2020). HSC Results.

OECD, (2011). PISA. In Focus 7. Private schools: Who benefits?

OECD, (2018). PISA 2018 Results.

OECD. (2023). Better Life Index.

Parliament of Australia. (2013). Australian Education Act 2013. Canberra. Australia.

Parliament of Victoria. (1994). The Financial Management Act 1994. Victoria. Australia.

Parliament of Victoria. (2004). The Public Administration Act 2004. Victoria. Australia.

Parliament of Victoria. (2006) The Education and Training Reform Act 2006. Victoria, Australia.

Parliament of Victoria. (2006). The Education and Training Reform Act Regulations 2007. Victoria. Australia.

Parliament of Victoria. (2011). Independent Broad-Based Anti-Corruption Commission Act 2011. Victoria. Australia.

Parliamentary Budget Office. (2020). Victorian Schools Determining and distributing funding. 2020.

Patty, A. (2019). Questions loom over legal validity of school funding. Sydney Morning Herald. January 27, 2019.

Patty, A. (2019). Funding Formula: The Complex Case of School Funding in Australia. The Sydney Morning Herald. https://www.smh.com.au/

Peck, J., & Theodore, N. (2015). Fast Policy: Experimental Statecraft at the Thresholds of Neoliberalism. University of Minnesota Press.

Phillips, J., & Lamont, A. (2014). Australian Political Parties in the Spotlight: Labor, Liberal and the Nationals. Parliamentary Library Research Paper.

Poisson, M. (2010). Corruption and Education. International Institute of Educational Planning: Paris

Pole, N. (1999). Formula Funding of Schools in New Zealand. In K. N. Ross, and R. Levacic (Ed.). Needs-based Resource Allocation in Education via Formula Funding to Schools. IIEP, Paris.

Potts, A. (1997). Public and Private Schooling in Australia – Historical and contemporary considerations. Institute of Historical research. University of London.

Productivity Commission. (2012). Schools Workforce. Research Report, Canberra: Productivity Commission.

Reid, A. (2012). Perspectives: Federalism, Public Education and the public goods. Whitlam Institute. University of Western Sydney. Australia.

Rhodes R. A. W. (Ed) (2009). The Australian Study of Politics, Palgrave and Macmillan.

Robertson, S. L., & Dale, R. (Eds.). (2015). Global Education Policy and International Development: New Agendas, Issues, and Policies. Bloomsbury Academic.

Rodríguez-Pose, A., & Gill, N. (2003). The Global Trend towards Devolution and Its Implications. Environment and Planning C: Government and Policy, 21(3), 333-351.

Rossmiller, Richard. (1994). Equity or adequacy of school funding. Educational Policy. Vol 8 No. 4 1994.

Rothstein, Jesse and Diane Whitmore Schanzenbach1. (2021). Does Money Still Matter? Attainment and Earnings Effects of Post-1990 School Finance Reforms August 2021.

Rowe, Emma (2017). Religion in Australian schools: an historical and contemporary debate. The Conversations.

Rubenstein, R., Doering, J., & Shapiro, R. (2000). Equity and Adequacy in State School Finance Distribution Formulas. National Tax Journal, 53(1), 9-26.

Sachs, J. (2001). Teacher professional identity: Competing discourses, competing outcomes. Journal of Education Policy, 16(2), 149-161.

Savage, Glenn C. (2019). What is policy assemblage? January 2019 Territory Politics Governance 8(3):1-17 January 20198(3):1-17. DOI:10.1080/21622671.2018.1559760

Savage, Glenn C.; and Gorur, R. (2013). Equity and marketisation: emerging policies and practices in Australian education. Article in Discourse Studies in the Cultural Politics of Education·

Save Our Schools. (2024). Australia's Resource Gaps: PISA 2022 Report Highlights Inequities. http://saveourschools.com.au/

Save Our Schools. (2024). Report on resource gaps and educational inequities in Australian schools.

Save Our Schools. http://saveourschools.com.au/

Seddon, Terri, Ed.; Angus, Lawrence, ed. (2000). Beyond Nostalgia: Reshaping Australian Education. Australian Education Review Series, No. 44.

Sherington, G., Campbell, C. (2004). Australian Liberalism, the middle class and public education from Henry Parkes to John Howard. Education research and Perspectives, Vol 31 No2 2004.

Spyros Themelis (ed). (2021). Critical Reflections on the Language of Neoliberalism in Education. First published 2021 by Routledge.

Starr, K. (2012). Above and beyond the bottom line: The extraordinary evolution of educational business management. Camberwell, Victoria: ACER Press.

Starr, K. (2015). Education game changers: Leadership and the consequences of policy paradox. Rowman & Littlefield.

State Service Authority. (2007). Code of Conduct for Victorian Public Sector Employees. Melbourne. Australia.

Statham, Audrey. (2014). Secular': an aspiration or a dirty word in Australian education? The Conversations.

Sunday Herald Sun. (2012). Thieves fleece schools. 25 March 2012. Page 27. Melbourne. Australia.

Sunday Herald Sun. (2014). Theft charge laid against former Brighton Secondary College business manager. 12 March 2014.

Sweetman, E, Long, C. R., and Smyth, J. (1922). A History of State Education in Victoria. The Education Department of Victoria. Melbourne. Australia.

The Age. (2012). Crime rife across Victoria's schools. 8 April 2012. Page 8. Melbourne. Australia.

The Age. (2023). Former Melbourne High business manager jailed over $430,000 theft. By Melissa Meehan. March 6, 2023.

The Australian. (2011a). Private school funding queried. 6 September 2011. Page 2. Melbourne. Australia.

The Australian. (2011b). State slams school's fund model. 5 November 2011. Page 3. Melbourne. Australia.

The Centre for public integrity. (2021). Protecting the integrity of accountability institutions: an independent funding model.

The Educator, (2023). Principals: how vulnerable are your school funds to fraud? by Brett Henebery 14 Mar 2023.

The Sunday Age. (2012). Staff, Parents Rort Schools: Documents Reveal Widespread Theft and Fraud. 29 January 2012.

Thompson, P. (2010). School leadership: Heads on the block?. Routledge.

Tomazin, F. (2014). Labour extends hand to "abandoned" schools. Sunday Age. 14 December 2014.

Tranter, D. (2018). Multiculturalism and Integration: A Harmonious Relationship. Springer.

Unceta, Alfonso and Medrano, Concepción. (2010). Equality, Equity, and Diversity: Educational Solutions in the Basque Country, Current Research Series No. 1. University of Nevada.

UNICEF. (2000). Defining Quality in Education. A paper presented by UNICEF at the meeting of The International Working Group on Education Florence, Italy June 2000.

United Nations Development Programme (UNDP). (2023). Human Development Index.

VanLehn, K. (2011). The relative effectiveness of human tutoring, intelligent tutoring systems, and other tutoring systems. Educational Psychologist, 46(4), 197-221.

Vesely, R. S., & Crampton, F. E. (2004). Equity and Adequacy in School Funding. In J. Guthrie (Ed.), Encyclopedia of Education (2nd ed.). Macmillan Reference USA.

Victorian Auditor General. (2016). Grants to Non-government schools. March 2016.

Victorian Competition and Efficiency Commission. (2013). Making the Grade: Autonomy and Accountability in Victorian Schools. State of Victoria. Melbourne. Australia.

Victorian Institute of Teaching. (2010). Annual Report 2010. Victorian Institute of Teaching. Melbourne. Australia.

Victorian Labour (2014). Victorian Labour Platform 2014, https://www.vicLabour.com.au.

Victorian Ombudsman. (2011). Corrupt conduct by public officials in procurement. Victorian government printer. Melbourne. Australia.

Victorian Ombudsman. (2020). Investigations into allegations of nepotism in government schools. 20 May 2020.

VRQA. (2023). New School Registration Briefing 20 March 2023.

Wambalaba, F. W., & Datta, S. (2018). The Impact of Artificial Intelligence on Student Learning in Higher Education. Journal of Higher Education Management, 33(1), 19-35.

Ward, I. (2006). Australian Political Institutions. Pearson Australia.

Weick, Karl E.(1976). Educational Organizations as Loosely Coupled Systems. Administrative Science Quarterly. Vol. 21, No. 1 pp. 1-19. Sage Publications, Inc.

Wested. (2000). From equity to adequacy. Policy brief. https://www2.wested.org/www-static/online_pubs/po-00-03.pdf. July 2000.

Whiteford, P. (2010). Australia: Inequality and Prosperity and Their Impacts in a Radical Welfare State. In G. Esping-Andersen (Ed.), The Three Worlds of Welfare Capitalism. Princeton University Press.

Whitty, Geoff, & Sally Power, (2002). The School, the State and the Market. v.2, n.1, pp. i-xxiii, Jan/Jun 2002.

Wicks, B. (1997). Understanding the Australian Constitution: the plain words. Libra Books, Sandy Bay Australia.

Wilkins, Andrew and Antonio Olmedo. (2019). Education Governance and Social Theory. Interdisciplinary Approaches to Research. Edited by Bloomsbury Academic. 2019. (selected one chapter for analysis.

Wilkinson, Ian R. et al. (2007). A History of State Aid to Non-Government Schools in Australia. Canberra: Commonwealth of Australia, DEST.

Wilkinson, Ian. (2013). State aid to non government schools – Australia 1788-2013. http://dehanz.net.au/wp-content/uploads/2013/12/State-aid1.pdf.

Williams, G., & Beck, L. (2020). The High Court and the DOGS Case: Revisiting the Constitutionality of Public Funding for Religious Schools. University of New South Wales Law Journal, 43(1), 93-111.

Zeide, E. (2017). The structural consequences of Big Data-driven education. Big Data, 5(2), 164-172.

Appendix 2

About the Author

Bandara Bandaranayake completed his B.Ed. (Honors) Degree and MPhil Degree from the University of Colombo. He earned his PhD at Monash University on a Monash Graduate Scholarship.

After obtaining his first degree, he joined the Ministry of Education in Sri Lanka and held several secondary school teaching positions before advancing to senior administrative roles in the Education Service. Following the completion of his PhD and a short tenure at Monash University, he joined the public service. Over three decades, he held several senior positions at the Department of Internal Affairs (New Zealand), the Department of Innovation, Industry and Regional Development (Australia), and the Department of Education (Australia).

His research interests include educational governance, ethics and integrity, public sector reforms, public policy, cultural anthropology, and evolutionary psychology. He has published several books and numerous journal articles.

Currently, he engages in independent research, consultancy, and counselling.

www.ingramcontent.com/pod-product-compliance
Lightning Source LLC
Chambersburg PA
CBHW071956290426
44109CB00018B/2040